PIANO TECHNIQUE

Tone, Touch, Phrasing and Dynamics

by Lillie H. Philipp

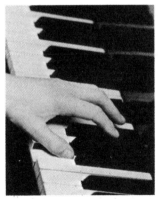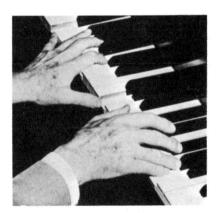

Dover Publications, Inc.
New York

Behind the mountains there live people, too. Be modest; as yet you have discovered and thought nothing which others have not thought and discovered before you. And even if you have done so, regard it as a gift from above, which you have to share with others.

Robert Schumann
Rules for Young Musicians

Published in Canada by General Publishing Company, Ltd., 30 Lesmill Road, Don Mills, Toronto, Ontario.
Published in the United Kingdom by Constable and Company, Ltd.

This Dover edition, first published in 1982, is an unabridged republication of the work originally published by MCA Music (a division of MCA Inc.), New York, in 1969 under the title *Piano Study: Application & Technique.*

International Standard Book Number: 0-486-24272-2

Manufactured in the United States of America
Dover Publications, Inc.
180 Varick Street
New York, N.Y. 10014

Library of Congress Cataloging in Publication Data

Philipp, Lillie H.
  Piano technique.

  Reprint. Originally published: Piano study: application & technique. New York: MCA Music, 1969.
  1. Piano––Instruction and study. I. Title.
[MT220.P615 1982]   786.3′041   81-15100
ISBN 0-486-24272-2   AACR2

preface

This book is an introduction to basic technique for all piano students. There is no simpler and more effective approach to piano playing than acquiring a thorough knowledge of the essentials, which are often overlooked in today's methodology. Technique does not really change with the times, but rather is expanded by the new music of each succeeding generation; thus there will always be the need to master the fundamental principles.

Piano Technique: Tone, Touch, Phrasing and Dynamics is a guide toward this goal. It is a working manual, containing technical studies, excerpts from piano works and photographs, all of which should be utilized by the student to develop a sound technique in a comparatively short time.

The technical studies may be practiced in as many keys as the student desires. He may make his own decisions as to which particular studies best serve his individual needs. Memorizing and practicing them without looking at the music is preferable. On very hot days, "loosening up" studies may be omitted. When the entire body is warm, the blood circulates more quickly and the fingers are naturally more nimble. With methodical practice, a good technique can easily be obtained.

While excerpts do not make the same demands upon the student as entire pieces, they will, however, familiarize him with different technical, stylistic and musical approaches. He will learn how to practice and what to look for when studying a piano work; he should repeat the excerpts over and over again, thus preparing himself for the eventual study of the entire work.

Hand positions in the photographs should be treated like studies. The student should apply them to his own hands and copy the indicated motions repeatedly.

The chapter "On Teaching Beginners" has been included because this area of piano pedagogy often suffers from diffuse thinking. No gimmick can ever replace the logical build-up which is necessary to launch the young student. Without individual attention, just as essential in class as in private instruction, the student's progress will be impeded. The principles contained in this chapter, as well as throughout the book, are derived from the author's lifetime experience.

The student will find many of Robert Schumann's quotations in this book. They are truly the great thoughts of a great pedagogue.

Lillie Herman-Philipp
Los Angeles, 1969

acknowledgments

The author wishes to express her indebtedness to her friend, Mrs. Geraldine Smith Healy, Supervisor of Music, Los Angeles City Schools, who generously gave of her time to edit the manuscript and without whose faith and encouragement this book might never have been written. Grateful acknowledgment is due Mr. Virgil Thomson who read the manuscript and whose suggestions proved invaluable. The author is also grateful to Mr. Alexander Borovsky and to Mr. Artur Rubinstein for supplying photographs of various hand positions.

The author wishes to acknowledge with thanks her appreciation for the helpful cooperation of the following individuals and institutions:

For biographical data: Mr. Nicholas Slonimsky; Mr. William Lichtenwanger of the Library of Congress, Music Division, Washington, D.C.; Mr. M. A. Jeffery, University of Toronto, Royal Conservatory of Music, Canada; Mr. Thor E. Wood, Chief, Research Library of the Performing Arts, New York Public Library; Mr. Frederick Freedman, Music Librarian, U.C.L.A.

For photographs: Mrs. Joelle Huss; Mr. Sol Hurok; Mrs. Lena Nilsen, Le Conte Jr. High School, Los Angeles; Mr. Cliff Paisley, Florida State University, Tallahassee.

For practical advice: Dr. Virginia Whitfield, University of Oregon; Miss Gerda Mora.

For proofreading: Mrs. Adelaide Tusler.

Photographs of the author and of the author's hands were taken by Fred Seligo. Graphics on the "Tree of Keyboard Masters" were done by Mr. Charles Roberts.

The author wishes to express her very special thanks to Mr. Lewis Roth, who organized this publication. It is through his guidance and assistance that the book is presented in this form.

contents

introduction

There has been need for a book which contains suggestions and examples for developing correct though varied piano playing techniques and a methodology for practicing according to the ideas of great teachers, past and present.

Lillie Herman-Philipp in her *Piano Technique: Tone, Touch, Phrasing and Dynamics* fulfills this need. Her book should prove to be a valuable reference guide for pupils and teachers in private and public schools.

Her emphasis on developing the proper playing skill and practicing technique is enhanced by the authentic and interesting treatment of problems concerned with the study of the piano.

The Tree of Keyboard Masters presents in chronological order the history of keyboard pedagogy from Bach to Rosina Lhévinne.

I am happy this book is now with us.

Geraldine Smith Healy
Supervisor of Music
Los Angeles City Schools

about the author

Lillie Herman-Philipp, a resident of Los Angeles since 1939 where she has been a well-known teacher of piano and lecturer in music, was born in Berlin of American parentage. There she was a piano student of Professor Moritz Mayer-Mahr, continuing her studies with Michael Zadora, a student of Busoni, and later in London with Moriz Rosenthal, a student of Liszt.

She has concertized, coached and accompanied singers for concerts in Berlin and London, working with, among others, Emanuel List and Walter Kirchoff of the Metropolitan Opera Company, Eleanor Marlow of the Chicago Opera Company, and Thea Bieber of the Berlin State Opera House. She has also supervised piano recordings in Paris, London and Berlin.

In Los Angeles, she has given institutes and piano workshops for music teachers in the city secondary schools under the auspices of the Los Angeles Board of Education. In addition to her teaching and lecturing, she has been active in promoting young talent through the Young Musicians Foundation, where she was a member of the board of trustees, as well as in other local organizations such as the Ojai Festivals.

chapter I

Seating Position

Except that it is several octaves longer, the keyboard is no different today than it was at the time of Couperin and Bach.

The student must first assure himself of the proper distance from the chair to the keyboard. The length of his forearm should be his guide. Hands and arms, if not forced into unsuitable positions, are relaxed, but sitting too close or too far from the keyboard forces them into the wrong positions.

The center of the piano is close to middle F, not middle C. Seated directly in front of the pedals, forearms raised, we find our fingers on the following notes:

A child's hands may not even be that far apart, thus:

If the seat is the correct height so that the elbow of the raised forearm is kept on the same level with the keyboard, the student will discover that in this natural position the elbow will be close but never pressed to the body.

The wrong chair height can influence the student's playing considerably. If he sits too low with the elbow below keyboard level, the fingers will have to work harder and the weight of the arm will become a burden; if he sits too high, his playing may become rigid and he will be unable to produce modulated tones. Only if the student is seated properly, on the front of the chair, with the body bent slightly forward, and with the arms hanging loosely from the shoulder, can he secure freedom of movement. When playing the higher or lower registers, the elbows should not be restrained or forced to remain close to the body.

Hand and Finger Positions

Before placing his hand on the keyboard, the student should turn it, shaping it as if he intends to hold an apple or a pear.

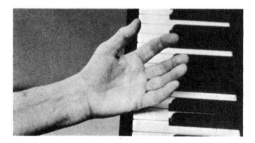

His hand and forearm will remain in one line; his wrist, flexible; his hand, curved; his thumb in a natural position; and his other fingers slightly curved inward.

When placing the fingers on the keyboard, the student must be sure that the second and fifth fingers are in the *center* of the *ivory keys* and that the contact between the little finger and the key will not be on the side of the finger.

With the second and fifth fingers in proper position, the third and fourth fingers will find their places automatically.

The Thumb,* Wrist, Elbows

Now we have four fingers on the keys and must next find the proper position for the thumb. In arching the hand, we adjust to each person's individual dimensions.

The short-fingered student should cup his hand less than the long-fingered student. The knuckles are pushed up by the fingers so that the first joint of the thumb can find its proper place with the side of the nail on the edge of the key. The arm must be relaxed; the wrist, flexible; the fingers, firm in a curved position.

As the student progresses, he will discover that the angle with which the thumb comes in contact with the key is bound to vary. If special passages, chords or octaves demand changes in hand position, the student may have to move the thumb further up on the ivory key in the direction of the black key.

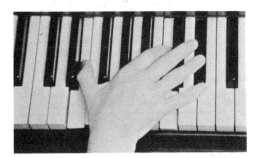

With the correctly-shaped hands on the keys, the student should keep the outside line of his hand, wrist and forearm as straight as possible. If this needs correction, he should shift his wrist.

There can be no absolute law for hand position since the dimensions of various hands differ so much. It was the great Busoni who took a firm stand against the would-be lawmakers. Tobias Matthay tried to create laws but failed.

The student can play on the cushions or the tips of his fingers. Both ways are correct.

  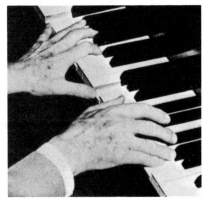

Ken Richards

*See pp. 22-27.   The hands of Ernst von Dohnanyi

In Bach's time, during the eighteenth century, when pianos had little volume and tones were of short duration, it was the general custom to play with a flat hand and flat fingers. Today, with pianos having a full volume, the pianist has to depend upon his skill to produce short tones.

The teacher must guide the student, consider the dimensions of his hands and never force them into unsuitable positions. If the thumb is too short compared to the length of the other fingers, as often happens, the student will be forced to play more on the tips than on the cushions of the fingers. Chopin and many others played on the cushions with outstretched fingers. Those who have seen the late Josef Hofmann play could not help but observe that he raised his fifth finger in the shape of a fishhook.

It is a wasted effort to restrain motions which come naturally. However, mannerisms must not be taken for motions; the former should be kept under control.

Depressed Knuckles, Collapsed Fingers

In the nineteenth century, Clementi, Cramer, Kullak and Nicholas Rubinstein taught piano playing with depressed knuckles without consideration for the hand's structure, a method which can easily create muscular tension.

The student should not consider it unfortunate if he plays with depressed knuckles, provided this is nature's doing and the structure of the hand is such that depressed knuckles come naturally.

Double-jointed or collapsed fingers, however, are detrimental, as the fingers must remain firm at all times. The student must work hard to overcome this tendency. Exercises will strengthen the fingers and bring them under command. Trill studies (pp. 19-20) are recommended.

From the contemporary descriptions, we know that "Bach placed his hands on the finger board so that his fingers were bent . . ."*

The Thumb

With mechanical progress in the development of instruments, it became more and more important to develop strong fingers. Although the thumb, the crucial finger, is the most adept, it seems to require our special attention.

Before Bach's time and during his lifetime, the thumb was used when the other fingers could not do the job without it, as, for example, in large stretches. Bach himself was an exception, being the first to use the thumb freely on both black and white keys. The normal function of the thumb as nature intended is to reach, grasp and hold an object which the other fingers cannot hold without its help. In contrast to the other fingers which function just one way, up and down, the thumb goes through two motions to depress a key: *sideways* and up and down.

Artur Rubinstein

*Forkel, Johann Nikolaus. *Johann Sebastian Bach.* Translated by Charles Sanford Terry, Harcourt, Brace & Howe. New York, 1920, p.50.

The thumb has to be taught to be in constant readiness either to move under the other fingers or to get out of the way. Observe the positions of the thumbs when depressing the second finger of the right hand and the third finger of the left hand.

1. Bartók: *Mikrokosmos*, Vol. IV, No. 98
m. 1-3

The thumb is a necessary adjunct and, at the same time, is inclined to be lazy — an unhappy combination. Therefore we invent exercises, anchoring alternate fingers, which the student should study at the beginning of each practice session, following up with other exercises and scales.

Uncontrolled movements of the elbow are certainly out of place and awkward looking. If the fingers are trained and well controlled, the student need not revert to antics with the elbow; the flexible wrist will do the turning.

2. Chopin: *Fantaisie-Impromptu,* Op. 66
m. 7

3. Liszt: *V. Sonetto del Petrarca*
m. 23

As mentioned in the section on hand position, we do not always play on dead center of the fingers. We may pivot or turn the finger tips so that the thumb has less distance to travel for smooth execution. To prepare the thumb for shifting under the hand, particularly for fast passage work or scales, we may want to turn slightly on each finger as if pivoting. Although the finger tips or cushions will be right over the keys, the keys will not always be struck from the same angle. The angle of the finger at impact will vary.

The more you turn the wrist in preparation for the thumb, the easier the shift will be. We use the wrist for this motion, and the thumb will hit the key partly with its nail and partly from the side.

5. Prokofieff: *Visions Fugitives*, No. 2
m. 7-9

6. Chopin: *Etude*, Op. 25, No. 2
m. 8

7. Chopin: *Etude*, Op. 10, No. 12
m. 10-11

Scales*

You must sedulously practice scales and other finger exercises. But there are many persons who imagine all will be accomplished if they keep on spending many hours each day, till they grow old, in mere mechanical practice. It is as if one should busy himself daily with repeating the ABC's as fast as possible, and always faster and faster. Use your time better.

Robert Schumann
Rules for Young Musicians

Practicing or playing without attentive listening is of no value. Even scales need our concentration and our ear's attention. The beginner should learn the scales right from the start. With the ingenious fingering we use today, they should be mastered just as the multiplication tables are, since only then will fingering for music in all keys come naturally. There is no better preparation for the performer and it is also good training for the ear.

Czerny, at the age of ten, became Beethoven's student and studied with him from 1800 to 1805. Beethoven required that he play the scales in all keys, also stressing the proper use of the thumb. In his autobiography Czerny writes: "In the first lessons Beethoven busied himself exclusively with the scales in all keys. He showed me many things that were then unknown to most players: the proper position of the hands and the fingers and the use of the thumb. Only much later did I recognize the full value of these rules."

Chopin, as well as Beethoven, stressed scales, moving from one note to the other over the entire keyboard. He demanded shifting the hand position with the keys and never striking a note before the finger was over the key. Scales and arpeggios had to be played by turning the hands inside (wrist motion).

In moving the wrists sideways, the fingers lie across the keys in a slanted position, which enables the thumb to move smoothly and prevents the scales from sounding rough. When learning a new scale, it is advisable to practice each hand separately so that the student gets a clear picture of the scale and wrong notes can be avoided. Only then should he proceed to play with both hands together.

The student should practice scales and exercises using accents to *overcome* uncalled-for accents. This requires that he play several times over the keyboard, with the accents falling on different notes each time. Practicing scales in this manner will strengthen fingers and develop controlled dynamics; also, the thumb will lose its prominence and become subordinate. However, the student should be beyond the beginning stage and already have some control over his fingers before practicing with accents. (See the section on the accent, p. 15.)

*See Examples, pp. 8-10.

When practicing scales and when giving *accent*

on every *third* note, play *four* octaves
on every *fourth* note, play *five* octaves
on every *fifth* note, play *six* octaves
on every *sixth* note, play *five* octaves
on every *eighth* note, play *five* octaves

Examples

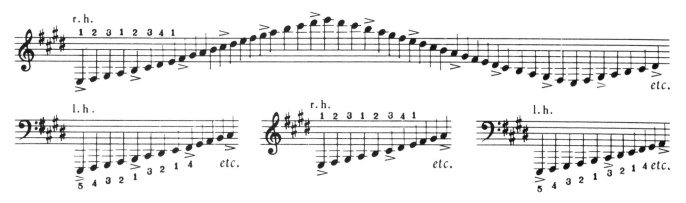

Scales can also be practiced with each hand separately, with varying accents and with the following fingering.

The professional may practice scales 20 to 30 minutes daily, according to his needs. The dedicated student should devote at least ten minutes daily to major, harmonic minor and melodic minor scales, practicing them in different styles – legato, staccato, piano, forte, fortissimo-staccato, and in thirds and sixths.

Never strain or become rigid. Keep your natural position with your body flexible, which will help to maintain a free wrist and floating elbow. The arm leads the finger to the next key. Do not be careless and play wrong notes; *be correct at all times.* Speed will develop gradually.

In carrying out these instructions, the student can provide his own variety. At one study session, for example, he may decide to practice two major scales and two minor scales, though there is no law against practicing more than two scales.

Suppose you have been practicing the F major scale with different accents and then continue with D minor. Without changing accents, you may want to play over the entire keyboard, once in the harmonic minor and the second time in the melodic minor. Or, you may play over three octaves once back and forth, the next time changing to five octaves, as long as you do not start and end with the accent on the thumb when having played *once* up and down, as the purpose then would be forfeited.

Another suggestion: concentrate on the left hand playing forte while the right hand plays pianissimo. Then reverse: play the right hand forte and the left hand pianissimo. Alternate dynamics. As a rule, we conquer passage work more easily with the right hand than with the left. Concentrate on your weaknesses and practice periodically with special concentration on the left hand.

After having practiced scales with accents, play them without accents. If you stumble, start slower and gradually increase speed. You can play scales as fast as you wish, provided you do not stumble and your ear tells you the dynamics are even and that you are playing in strict rhythm.

Examples

1. Parallel motion.

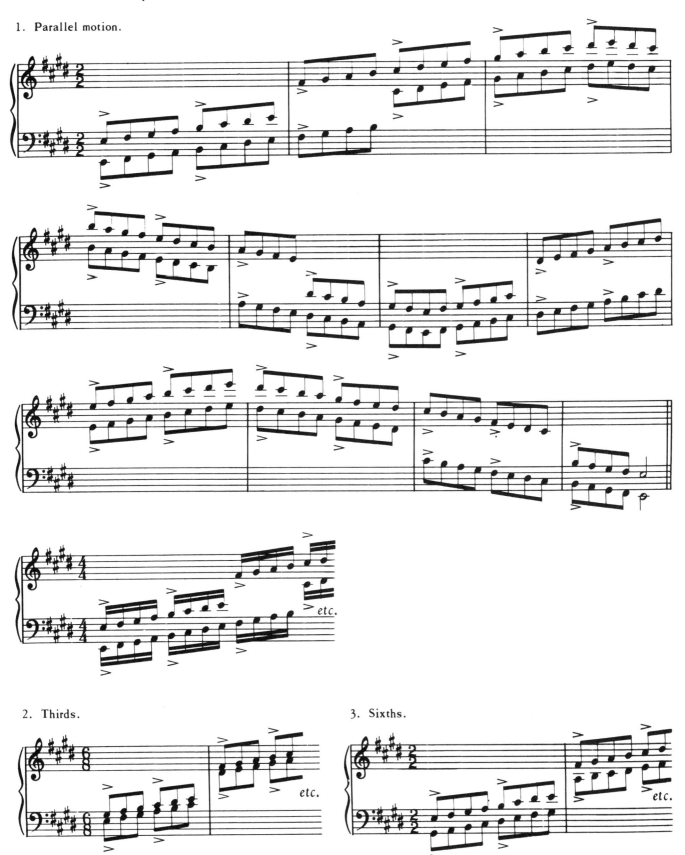

2. Thirds.

3. Sixths.

4. Three against two.

5. Two against three.

6. Four against three.

7. Three against four.

chapter II

Weight of Arm

One must differentiate between mass and weight. Mass is matter in bulk; weight is the amount of pressure a body exerts upon any support. The mass of the arm is unchangeable, whereas we have control over the weight through our muscles. The strength of the tone, its duration, its penetrating power, depend on the speed with which we hit the keys. The main proponent of the weight of arm method was Ludwig Deppe (1828-1890), a conductor by profession, but also one of the outstanding piano pedagogues of his time. Deppe's contemporaries, Kullak and Tausig, did not teach this method. We surely cannot look for it in the eighteenth century or the early nineteenth century, when pianos had a small volume of sound.

The position at the keyboard is described in Chapter I. The arm hangs loosely from the shoulder, fingers curved. The weight of the arm is raised to the keyboard; you feel the weight of your shoulders, evenly supplied, in the finger tips. There may be a slight bend in your wrist which need not be corrected.

Since you are completely relaxed, you will certainly not raise your fingers high. Your common sense must tell you that it is very tiring, if not impossible, to lift the fingers high with the weight of the arm bearing down on them.

Legato will be easier to achieve and will sound smooth if you listen carefully to the duration of each individual tone played. When playing with weight of arm, it is of the utmost importance that the finger should release the tone immediately, as soon as the next tone has been played, so as to avoid overlapping which destroys clarity.

8. Beethoven: *Rondo*, Op. 51, No. 2
m. 31-34

Andante cantabile e grazioso ♪= 96

Fingers must always be curved inward firmly but never too strongly since one will lose the sensitive feeling of the tips or cushions.

The forearm will gain prominence as one discovers that it is the guiding vehicle, and instead of giving shoulders any further thought, one will concentrate on hands, fingers and forearm. As the student will undoubtedly reason that it may be more tiresome for the fingers to support the weight of arm, he should make use of this weight with moderation.

Using only weight of arm can become very monotonous, but it is very useful in producing a single tone, and for passages that demand even dynamics, as in Beethoven, it is unsurpassed.

9. Schumann: *Fantasiestücke*, Op. 12, "Warum."
m. 1-2   **Langsam und zart** ♩= 56
Slow and tender

12

10. Beethoven: *Sonata*, Op. 31, No. 1
m. 30-45

Allegro vivace

You may use this touch in one hand while the other goes along without emphasis on weight. One hand may be light-fingered and the other heavy, using weight just for individual tones.

11. Chopin: *Fantaisie-Impromptu*, Op. 66
m. 43-45 **Moderato cantabile**

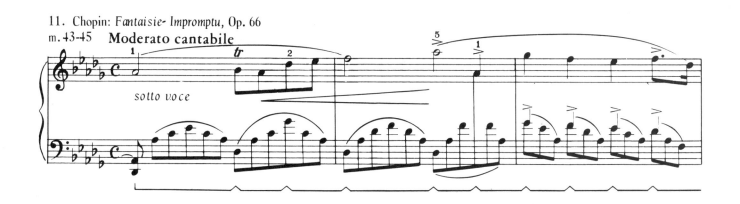

12. Rachmaninoff: Élégie, Op. 3, No. 1.

m. 41-46

With controlled weight of arm you obtain more nuance, a greater variety of shading at the finger tips, as it is easy to make tones sing with a flexible wrist and with weight. The tones will sound round and full, never hard or harsh. If you learn to use the pedal correctly in connection with the singing tone, you can achieve wonders. The slightest unevenness can be detected if you listen unceasingly to the tones as they are played. In no time, your "watchdog," the ear, will be your strongest critic and ally. For a perfect legato, one tone must be carried over to the next one, so that no one finger gets prominence over another.

Last but not least, for fortissimo octaves and chords, where power and strength alone may not be sufficient, the weight of the entire arm thrown into the piano will not only get the effect desired, but the tone will have a penetrating power you cannot achieve in any other manner. You literally take the chord into the hand before you throw it into the piano. A contemporary writes in one of his letters to a friend: "Liszt's hands were always in the air [fingers in position] striking the keys from above and very, very seldom hitting a wrong note."

13. Liszt: *Rhapsodie XII*

m. 14-16

14

14. Liszt: *Rhapsodie hongroise* No.15, "Rákóczi March"
m. 14-22

Tempo di Marcia animato

I believe that Liszt combined his percussive touch with the weight of his arm. His chords were literally thrown into the piano with a penetrating power.

The student who will familiarize himself with weight of arm playing must experiment on his own, and thus come to understand when and when not to use it.

The Accent*, Controlled Dynamics

If dynamics are under perfect control, there is no unevenness. If the fingers are not under perfect control, one will hear accents where none belong. And who enjoys hearing misplaced accents produced by the thumb, or what is just as bad, effects of weakness produced by the fourth or fifth finger? The restrained action of the fourth and fifth fingers influences the independence of the other fingers and is a foremost technical weakness of many. If by nature all fingers had equal strength and all muscles and ligaments had equal flexibility, technique would be easy to attain.

The beauty of a good performance lies in controlled dynamics. Practice with accents, using exercises, scales and pieces. Accents are to music what shadow and light are to painting. Concentrated studies will train hands and fingers and the constant attention of the mind.

When practicing scales or exercises with accents, each finger gets its turn. The accent falls on a different finger each time, which strengthens the fingers and helps to create controlled independence. The accent is given with the free-acting wrist and the weight of the forearm, which will influence the activities of the fingers and help to develop a supple hand. If you give the accent only with your finger, you might be inclined to raise the finger too high, producing a harsh tone instead of a full and round tone.

To try and equalize the strength of the fingers is practically impossible. Practicing with accent is your self-imposed control. It will be of great value to practice pieces as well as exercises and scales in the same manner.

When working on a piece, accent the first beat of each measure or every other measure. Gradually, the more the piece develops, the less pronounced will be the accents; gradually they will disappear and you will discover that you have created highlights. Besides, practicing with accents will keep wrists relaxed and flexible, and you will not tire.

*See Scales, Chapter I, and Studies, pp. 19-37.

15. Mozart: *Sonate,* K. 457

m. 1-8

Beethoven made extensive use of *sforzando* in his compositions. He wanted special notes or chords played with emphasis to create highlights — the very thing you, in turn, create by practicing with accents.

16. Beethoven: *Sonate,* Op. 53, (Waldstein).

m. 28   m. 66

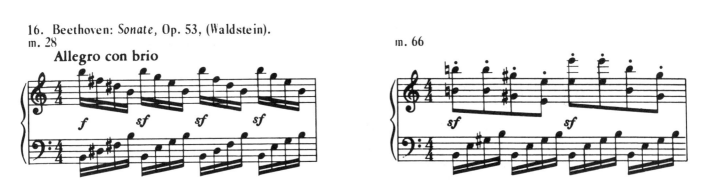

17. Beethoven: *Sonate,* Op. 57, (Appassionata), II Movement.

m. 49 - 50

m. 53 - 54

Massaging Exercises

It is advisable to massage the fingers before starting to practice so that the blood rushes through them faster. On very hot days you will not need these preparations. As you must have discovered for yourself, when your entire body is warm, your fingers will practically run away with you.

Stretch: Push the closely-held-together second, third, and fourth fingers of the right hand between the knuckles of the second and third fingers of your left hand, rubbing them rapidly in a clockwise and counter-clockwise motion. You will feel the stretch and warmth. Use the identical massage between the third and fourth fingers and the fourth and fifth fingers. Reverse this procedure for the other hand.

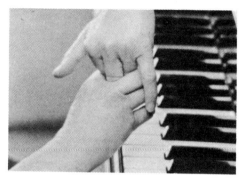

With stretch exercises, we are setting into motion a part of the hand that is neglected. If we stretch our arms and hands, we flex the muscles and stretch our fingers. We must exercise the muscles which we usually neglect.

Stretch Exercises at the Piano: Holding straight the wrist, hand and fingers of one hand, spread the second and third fingers apart. Depressing notes C and F or G, push the fingers up into the keys so that you feel the stretch.

Then, keeping the fingers in the stretched position, turn the palm of the hand first to one side, then to the other.

Repeat this motion several times and proceed to the other fingers, the third and fourth as well as the fourth and fifth. If, for the fourth and fifth fingers, the distance from C to F or G is too great, use C to E. You cannot enlarge the space between the fingers, but this exercise will help to keep the fingers supple and flexible. Stretch with moderation and never force the fingers *too far apart*. However, you should feel a *slight pull*.

Rub the knuckle of each individual finger in a clockwise and counter-clockwise motion good and hard several times. (You cannot hurt yourself.) The thumb and second finger will do the job.

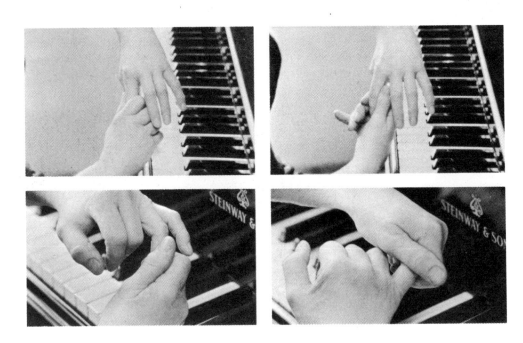

With the thumb and second finger of one hand, grip each finger of the other hand separately and rotate it firmly in its socket several times. (Loose rotation is useless.) *Never pull* your fingers or joints, as it can be harmful.

Finger rolling exercise without the thumb: Curb the tightly-held-together four fingers of one hand into a fist. Push them into the palm of the other hand, rapidly roll the fingers up and down and alternate hands. This is an excellent loosening up exercise.

Trill Exercises

At the piano: Trill exercises and anchoring one finger. (These can be considered the King Studies.) Exercises with accents through the wrist. The accent, executed with weight of arm, will necessitate a free-acting wrist. Wrist down for each accent given.

Alternate hands after each individual exercise, devoting more time to especially weak fingers. The following exercises can be practiced one octave higher or lower and extended over one octave or more. Since it is the student's aim to hold the wrists and elbows free, he can start his exercises on any tone that is convenient. The anchored finger must be kept down constantly.

Trill Studies

1. **First and second finger. Accent on first finger.**

2. **Second and first finger.**

3. **Second and third finger.**

4. **Third and second finger.**

5. **Third and fourth finger.**

6. **Fourth and third finger.**

7. Fourth and fifth finger.

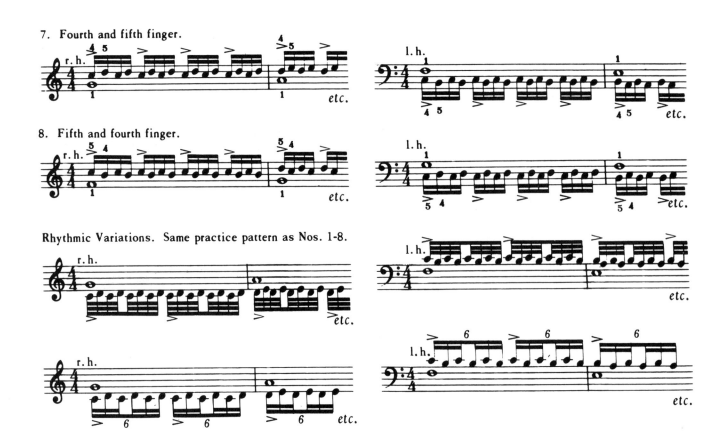

8. Fifth and fourth finger.

Rhythmic Variations. Same practice pattern as Nos. 1-8.

Chromatic Variations. Same practice pattern as Nos. 1-8. These studies may be shortened to five measures.

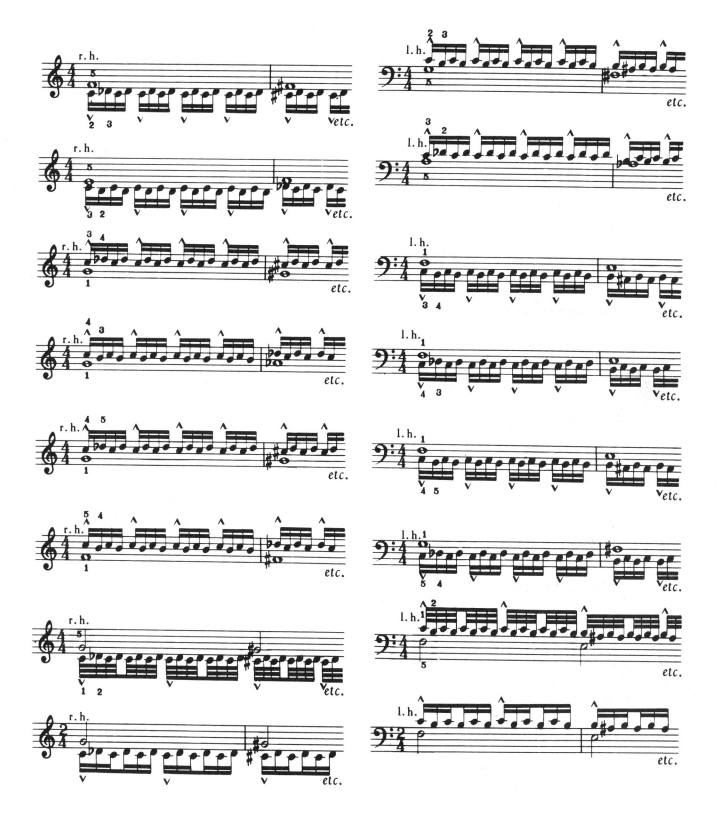

Thumb Exercises: These exercises are to be practiced with utmost relaxation and a flexible wrist; the elbow shall not be restrained and may move away from the body. Repeat exercises with multiple fingerings, each repetition using alternate fingers.

(Note: Diamond-shaped notes are to be depressed silently.)

The preceding may be studied with anchored thumb and reverse fingering.

Example:

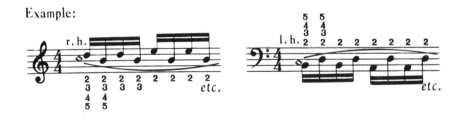

2. Chromatic Variations on Study No.1. Same pattern. Also to be practiced with reverse fingering.

3. The same pattern as Nos. 1 and 2, without anchored finger. These exercises will train the thumb to move smoothly and train the fingers to move easily over the thumb.

Four-Finger Exercises without the Thumb: This forces you to lift the fingers. If there is a tendency toward overlapping, start these exercises staccato. E major is the easiest scale. Then proceed legato to other keys, extending them over as many octaves as you wish. Give the accent with the weight of the arm. This will "break" the wrist and force you to work the fingers. The four-finger exercises, with their ever-changing accents, will strengthen the fingers and develop independence. They should also be practiced over four or more octaves without accents and as fast as possible. To give the fingers a higher fall, the outer edge of the hand should be held high. The wrist motion will then turn the hand out.

Note the high fall of the 5th finger.

1.

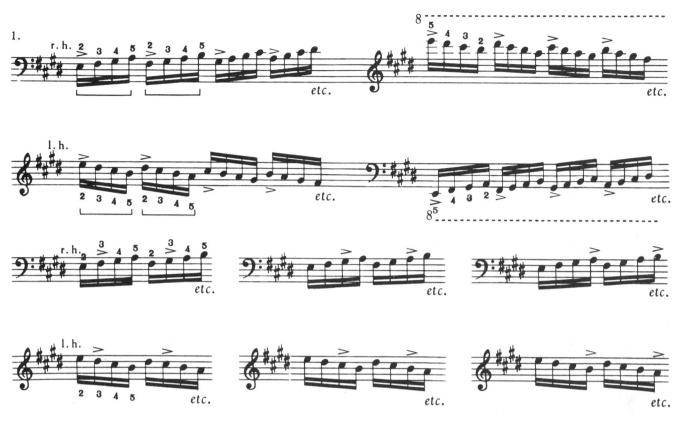

Studies 1 and 2 are also to be played without accents and as fast as possible.

2.

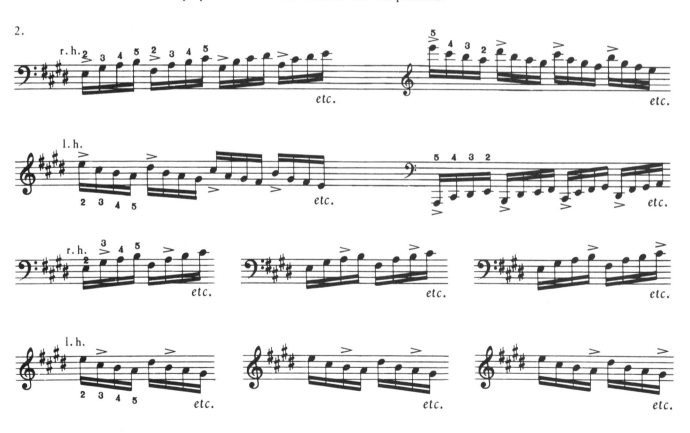

If the student is pressed for time and has to limber up his fingers in a hurry, the trill exercises, the four-finger exercises and the thumb exercises are recommended.

Exercises in Progressive Difficulty

1.

2.

3. Studies Nos. 3 and 4 to be played as fast as possible.

4.

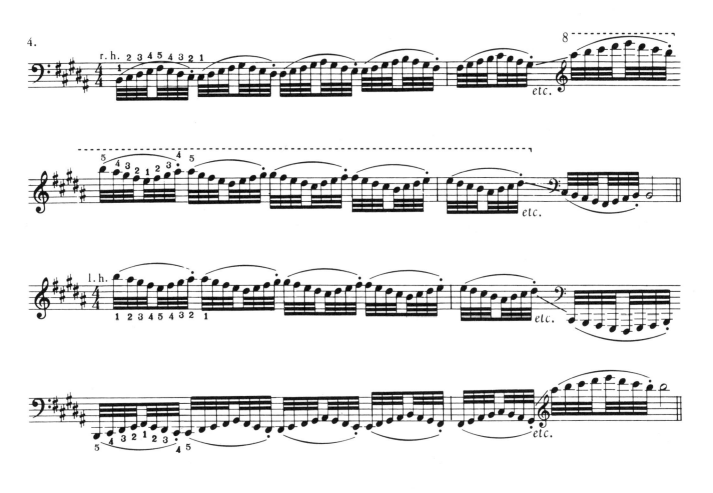

Studies with accent on fourth and fifth fingers.

1.

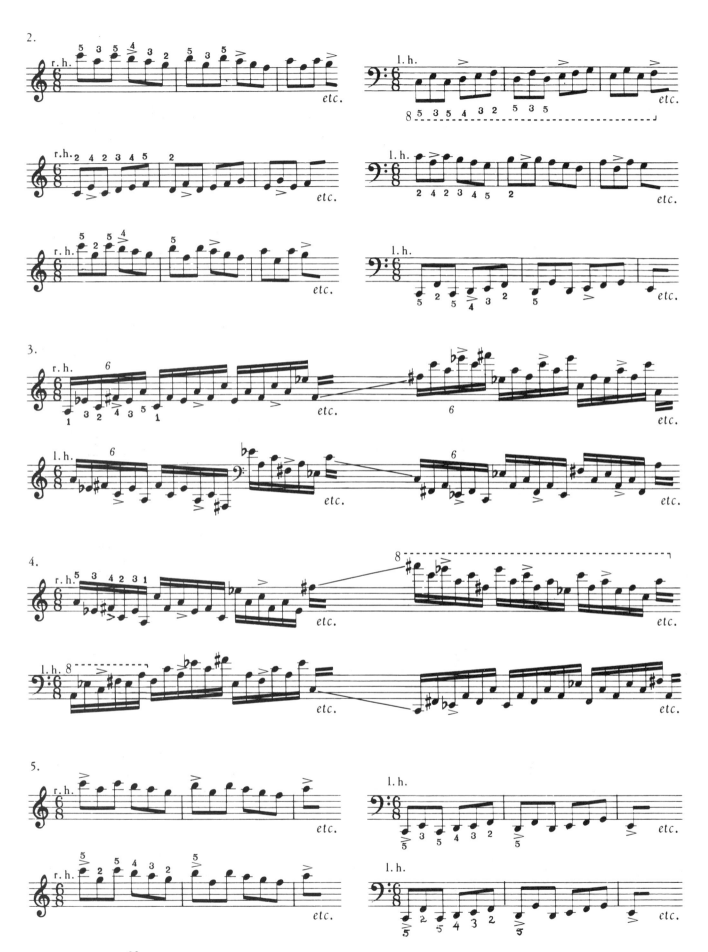

32

Broken Chords.

1.

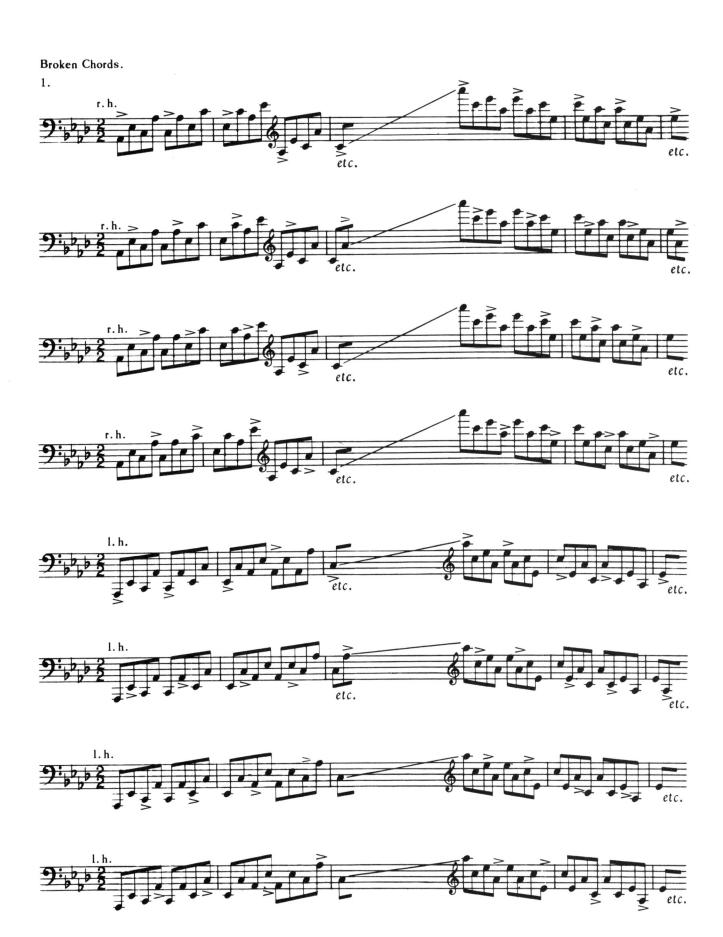

33

2.

3. Broken Chords with stretch.

Minor

Major

Minor   Major

6. This study to be played as fast as possible.

Skips and Leaps.

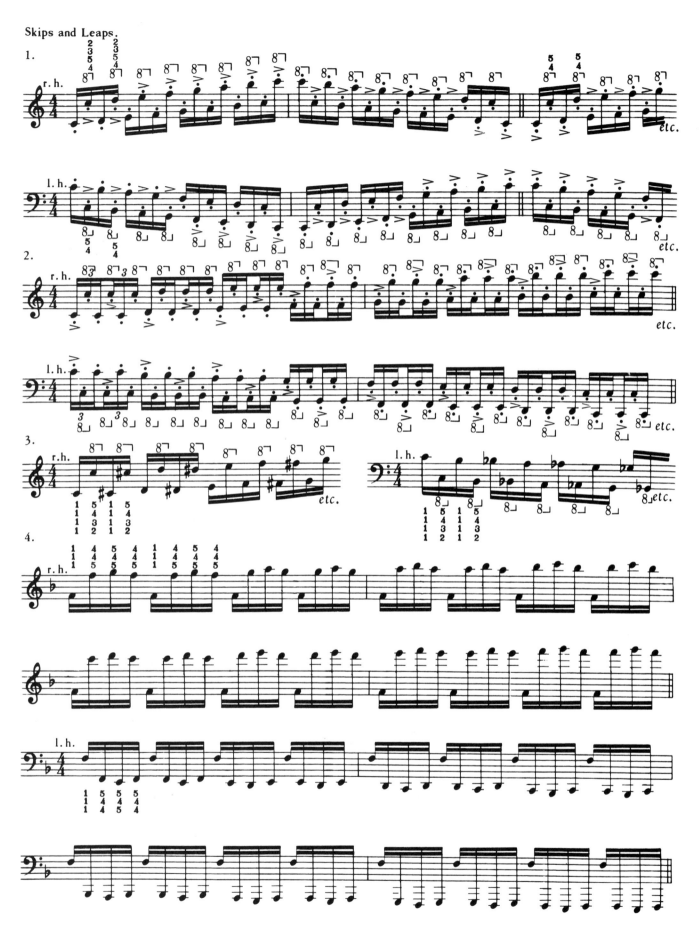

8. Brahms *Sonata*, Op. 2, in F# minor.
Measures 3-6 lend themselves well as studies for leaps for the right hand.

These bars can be broken up, repeated, and developed in any manner the student desires. See examples below.

Examples

Etudes

Piano etudes are generally pedagogical pieces of music of short or long duration, written for the purpose of furthering technical ability and preparing the student for piano literature. Alkan,* the French pianist and pedagogue, wrote some which last as long as fifteen minutes.

It is the belief of many pedagogues that students cannot start too early to study the etudes of Carl Czerny.** Czerny's etudes are good schooling for velocity and for fingering. Opus 740 was written for advanced students, stressing interpretation as well as speed. Opus 299 likewise stresses speed.

Czerny's *School of the Virtuoso*, Opus 365, advises the student to repeat some exercises thirty times. I advise against this since endless repetitions can improve the performance only if they are done attentively, and practicing without an observing ear will feed a poor memory.

It is hard to remain attentive after ten repetitions, although this is an individual thing. After repeating an etude five times without stumbling and without looking at one's hands, the tempo can then be increased and the etude played twice more. If the student does not improve, he should repeat the procedure the next day and continue to do so until he is able to increase the tempo without stumbling.

Once the student has mastered the etudes in correct tempo, there is no need to continue working on them, though it can do no harm if he repeats them once or twice a month.

Cramer's† etudes have always been popular, although they do not create any problems. He avoided runs as much as possible and seldom wrote beyond the middle of the keyboard.

For the advanced student, Henselt's Etude Opus 2, No. 6 will always be enjoyed.

18A. Henselt: *Etude, Op. 2, No. 6, "Si oiseau j'étais, à toi je volerais"*
m. 1-7

* Alkan, Charles Henri Valentin, 1813-1888.

** Carl Czerny was born in 1791, the year that Mozart died.

†Johann Baptist Cramer, born 1771, one year later than Beethoven.

18B. *Ibid.* Godowsky's transcription

Allegro *Con leggierezza, quasi zeffiroso* ♩. = 63

Preparatory Studies

Ignaz Moscheles' etudes are recommended. They are a transition from school etudes to concert etudes. The next step should be the Chopin etudes, which are, and most likely will always remain, the best of all etude literature.

19. Moscheles: *Etude*, Op. 70, No. 3. m. 1-3.
A chromatic study, interspersed with double notes.

20. Chopin: *Etude*, Op. 10, No. 2. m. 1-4
A chromatic study, interspersed with chords.

Observe position of third finger.

Liszt wrote twelve etudes in the form of exercises, all of them forerunners for his *Etudes d'execution transcendante.*

For the student who intends to make piano study his career, Chopin's and Liszt's etudes are concert material and demand systematic study. Otherwise, etudes should be selected to fit individual needs.

In Kabalevsky's *Twenty-four Preludes,* Opus 38, we detect the pedagogue. No. 6, if studied like an etude, disregarding the demanded tempo (Allegro molto), is excellent practice for the free-acting as well as for the anchored thumb. With the exception of four measures it is written in broken chords throughout. It is a very effective piece, and if practiced in the suggested fashion, can be mastered to perfection.

21. Kabalevsky: *Prelude,* Op. 38, No. 6
m. 6 - 11

Allegro molto

Piano literature is rich in good etudes for all grades. To include them in one's practice sessions will improve velocity and sight-reading ability. They should be practiced with dynamic changes; the fingering demands the utmost attention, and when the student masters them, he is well on the road.

chapter III

Without enthusiasm nothing real comes of art.

Robert Schumann
Rules for Young Musicians

Tone, Touch

Through years of attentive playing and practicing, conscientious students develop a sensitivity to tone, or rather, the speed with which the hammer strikes.

Hermann Helmholtz, the great physiologist and physicist, claimed that tone color changes with the varying speed of the hammer. The hammer, after leaving its bed, moves either fast or slow, correspondingly producing loud or soft tones. The dynamic value depends on the speed with which the key is struck. If the hammer strikes at a constant speed, the color of the tone will remain the same.

If a pianist's playing does not create any emotional reaction in the listener, if he "leaves the listener cold" (a phrase we hear repeatedly), it may be the result, to a great extent, of poor touch or strike control. Neither the clever Josef Hofmann nor Leopold Godowsky, two great pedagogues and pianists, ever mention tone production in their writings; Carl Czerny does not speak of it either. Through combination of different intensities, simultaneously or in succession, one can produce all the beautiful effects which we attribute to the secret of touch. My definition is the following: THE VARYING SHADES OF TOUCH OR STRIKE INTENSITY ARE TONE PRODUCTION.

To improve tone production, the student has to listen attentively to the tonal effect he is producing. He has to constantly analyze and try again and again to produce tones which have the intensity he wants.

The fingers are under the command of the brain and the sensitive ear. In turn, it is up to the fingers to be in command of the keyboard and to control tone duration and strength. We really have three split-second commands from the *brain, ears* and *fingers.* In the master pianist, they function simultaneously.

Artur Rubinstein

Copyright, Karsh, Ottawa

The student's ear will gradually respond and learn to control the intensity of the tone, and with it the fingers will respond automatically.

Good tone and touch can be created with curved fingers, with weight or without weight. It can also be produced by playing on the cushions of the fingers held comparatively straight, *à la* Chopin.

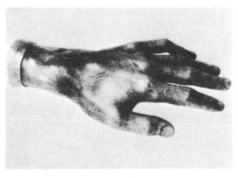

Chopin's left hand

Czeslaw Olszewski
Courtesy Instytut Fryderyca Chopina, Warsaw

You cannot produce a beautiful or an ugly single note, but with a combination of tones, you can make your piano playing sound beautiful and make your piano sing. The ears control the intensity of the tone, and the sensitivity of the fingers will learn to respond the more the student progresses.

It is not easy to get a good tone from the piano when sitting with the elbows above key level. But, for a "slappy" touch, where you may want to create atmosphere and color, as in Debussy and Ravel, this may be perfectly in order. Debussy's *Jardins sous la pluie* lends itself well to this approach, as does the opening page of Ravel's *Sonatine*. However, you can also produce a "slappy" touch while retaining your normal position at the piano, with elbows at key level.

The tone of the piano diminishes rapidly. However, there are times where we can take advantage of this and create fine special effects, as in short motives.

22. Mendelssohn: *Spring Song*, Op. 62, No. 6
m. 1-4

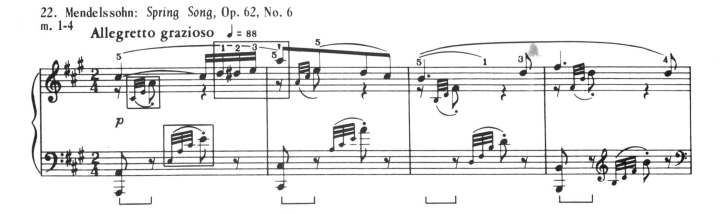

44

23. Emil Sauer: *Boîte à musique, (Spiel uhr)*

m. 1-5　**Tempo giusto**

una corda
automaticamente

senza Ped.

With the consent of Messrs. B. Schott's Söhne, Mainz

Antoine de Kontski, a contemporary of Chopin undoubtedly influenced by his teachings, wrote *L'indispensible du pianiste*. His method went to the extreme of recommending playing with straight fingers and low wrist. It was his belief that touch with the cushions of the fingers makes variation in shading much easier. He also recommends *carezzando* for *pianissimo* passages.

A *staccato* passage (detached notes) can be played with the tips of the fingers. One can also strike the keys as if dusting them, the fingers hitting the palm of the hand. I prefer a staccato played with the forearm where the fingers are practically motionless. With the released weight of the forearm, the fingers depress the keys and then release them immediately (half tone, half silence), in *fortissimo* or *pianissimo*, in any strength desired. The strength is controlled by the height from which your forearm is released. Very fast *staccato* is played with the fingers.

Staccatissimo, one-fourth sound and three-fourths silence, shall be played as short as possible.

For *mezzo staccato*, the finger should rest on the key, depress the key and release it immediately, employing the forearm with a flexible wrist for this motion.

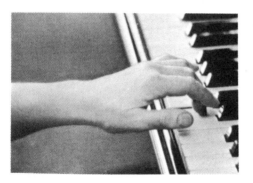 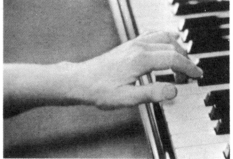

It is far easier to play loud notes in the bass with the left hand than in the treble with the right hand. It does not take much effort to overemphasize the bass, with or without weight. We will come across this fault frequently, not only in students.

Chords

Special attention has to be given to chord playing. If the dynamics of the fingers are not under strict control, the longer fingers may produce more tone than the shorter ones. This produces uncalled-for overtones. The coloring of a chord is changed by playing one of its component tones louder than the others. If we play the top note louder, the chord sounds brilliant; if we bring out the bass, it will sound warmer; but if one of the middle tones comes out most strongly, the sound will be harsh. A chord may sound ugly and sloppy if the tones are not played strictly together. However, taken in even arpeggio, the chord sounds full and rich.

No. 24 Chopin: *Etude,* Op. 10, No. 8
Final 2 measures

A good way of playing arpeggios (broken chords) is to use the weight of your arm with a rolling motion.

25. Grieg: *Concerto,* Op. 16, A minor
m. 3

stringendo

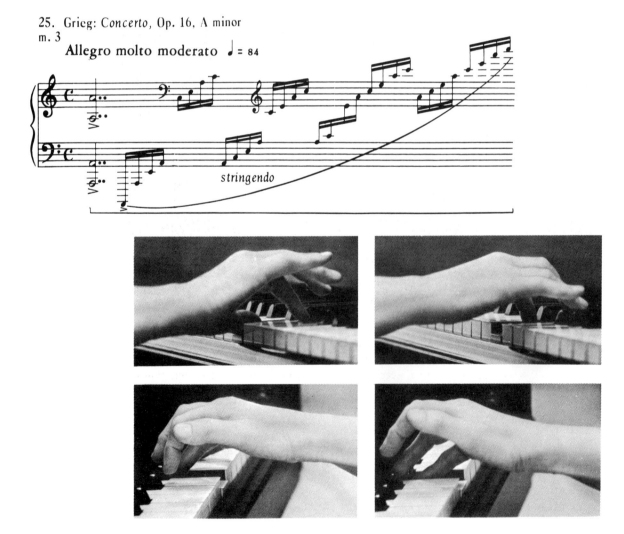

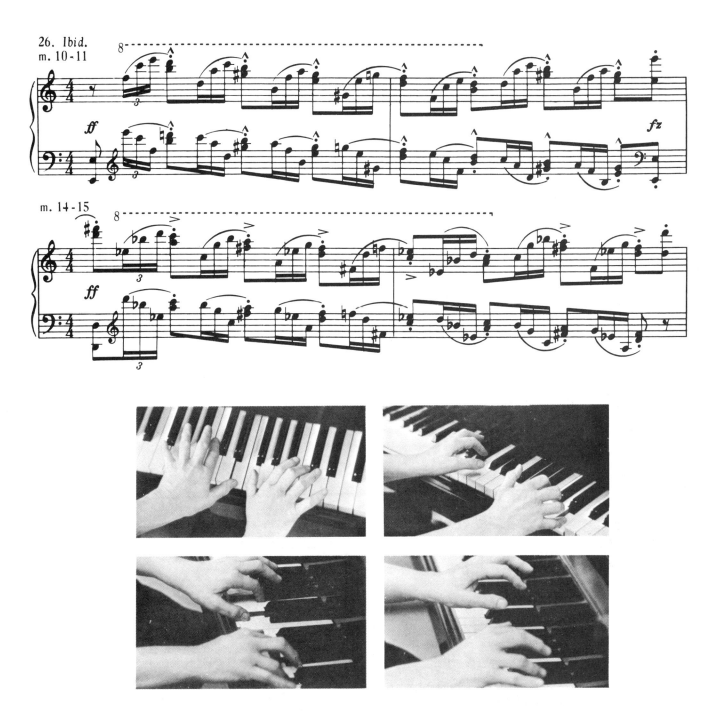

26. Ibid.
m. 10-11

m. 14-15

If the student knows that there are no secrets of touch, he will intensify his study to master his control of dynamic effects. Listening to his own playing will be of the greatest help to him.

If you want a melody to sing, keep the accompanying figuration softer and you will get the desired effect.

27. Chopin: *Nocturne, Op. 27, No. 2.*
m. 1-5

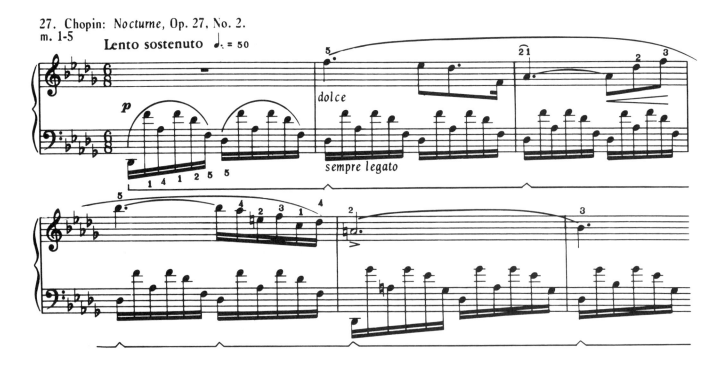

In spite of the two slurs in the first bar, the pedal can be held if the indicated fingering is used.

28. Schumann: *Widmung* (Dedication). Liszt's transcription
m. 1-7

The melody, as well as part of the accompaniment, is carried in one hand.

48

The Critical Ear

Always play as if a master heard you.

Robert Schumann
Rules for Young Musicians

When practicing, do you listen with a critical ear? You will undoubtedly hear it if you have struck a wrong note. But the student should realize that he must demand more from himself than just observing wrong notes.

With carelessness and negligence, you mistreat your ears. A student who makes demands on himself will be thorough and obey the commands of his ears; the sense of hearing needs as intensive training as the fingers and should be developed systematically. The student should listen to tone strength and duration and learn the control of tone shading. Only then can perfection be attained.

Rhythm is *not* controlled by the ear. You form a pattern and follow through; you can even be completely deaf and march in rhythm.

What is rhythm without tones, and what are tones without rhythm? Rhythm is order in movement. Time is an abstract quality, yet timing and tempo are anything but abstract.

Music is a demanding master, asking for more than controlled rhythm and different degrees of speed. It makes demands on the soul, the ear, and *the brain*. The fingers will execute what the brain orders but the brain must know what to order. Practicing without concentrating the thoughts and the ear on each note is a waste of time. The student can only control exact execution if he has trained himself to hear correctly.

You need the ear also for inspiration, but before you can afford the luxury of being carried away by the sounds you are producing, the ear must be trained to continuous self-hearing. There are times when a student may have to limit his powers. When performing for a small group in a private salon, uncontrolled bravura would be acoustically out of place.

Reflect early on the tone and character of different instruments; try to impress the peculiar coloring of each upon your ear.

Robert Schumann
Rules for Young Musicians

chapter IV

If I do not practice for one day I will hear it.
If I do not practice for two days my friends will hear it.
If I do not practice for three days the audience will hear it.

Hans von Bülow

Practicing and Fingering, Chromatic Scales

Every music student has the desire to acquire a good, reliable technique. If truly dedicated, he will work diligently since he knows that there can be no excellence without effort. In acquiring a good technique, reliable fingering is essential.

We regard the thumb as the first finger, the index finger as the second, and so on. (In some old music the thumb is marked "O" and the other fingers marked as for string instruments, the index finger being number one, and so on.)

When studying a new composition, professional and non-professional alike will first work out a fingering that is best suited to them. It will assist memorization to make fingering notations on the music itself. I have seen music with different fingerings written one on top of the other, and this by accomplished pianists. Why might one change fingering over and over again? Because fingering that is comfortable for slow playing need not necessarily be satisfactory for a fast tempo. The student should be very definite in deciding on his fingering, as a haphazard one can be disastrous.

"While playing always think ahead of the approaching notes; for these often necessitate modification of a normal fingering."*

One should practice slowly so as to avoid stumbling, only gradually increasing speed until he is able to play in the right tempo without faltering. Stumbling will tell you that you are playing too fast, that your fingers have not been sufficiently prepared for the required tempo or that you may not have repeated the passage often enough. How often must you repeat? This is individual. No matter in what tempo you play, you should always attempt to play in absolute equality of time. Reading carefully and accurately, practice from hand position to hand position and from phrase to phrase.

How does one attain speed? One prepares for it gradually, by practicing slower than the required tempo until the fingers find their place in an increased speed. However, you must avoid playing too slow or dragging. Once you know the piece, keep up the right tempo since there is no longer any need to play it slower. It is also unnecessary to play slower than the power of concentration demands.

Dragging and hurrying are equally great faults.

Robert Schumann
Rules for Young Musicians

* C.P.E. Bach: *Essay on the True Art of Playing Keyboard Instruments,* edited by William J. Mitchell, W. W. Norton & Co., New York, 1948, p. 44.

If you have made a mistake, correct it immediately. This will help your memory. It is senseless to repeat pages over and over after one has mastered them; unless one wants to improve phrasing, it is a waste of time.

One may often wonder why, after having mastered a piece, we do not always play it well. We may stumble. Why is that? This will happen to everyone, master and student alike, and it does not necessarily mean that difficult runs or passages have not been sufficiently prepared. It may simply mean that the fingers at this moment are not limber enough. The answer is: condition your fingers. Be sure that your fingers are warm. (Josef Hofmann used to say he preferred a pot of hot water to exercises.) Revert to exercises to get them to obey you instead of working over and over a piece that you know. Often, however, without preparation but knowing that your fingers are at your command, you may tackle a piece you have not looked at in a long time and play it perfectly.

For reviewing older pieces in one's repertoire, the student should play from the music even if he knows it from memory. Otherwise how can one check to see if mistakes have crept in?

It is not advisable to practice each hand separately since we play with ten fingers and not just with two hands. One may have to go over each hand separately in certain places to assure correct reading, but the normal procedure is to practice with both hands together.

For pieces, the student should use the most advantageous, the easiest fingering. However, for exercises and in practicing passage work, the most difficult fingering is advised. Much time is wasted in ineffective practicing.

The student may at times consider different finger and hand positions; in changing from Bach's rounded fingers to Chopin's straight ones, we will use different muscles.

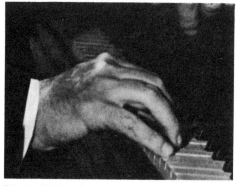

Eliascheff, New York

Alexander Borovsky's hand
Rounded fingers

29. Bach, J.S.: *The Well-Tempered Clavier*, Vol. I
Preludio X m. 1-2

Fuga X m. 1-3

Sviatoslav Richter's hands
Extended fingers

30. Chopin: *Etude*, Op. 19, No. 8. m. 1-2

Also, practicing pianissimo, as many great pianists have been known to do, will help to further technique and improve velocity.

Fingering for Chromatic Scales (Czerny)

For a fast tempo, the following fingering can be recommended:

Fingering for chromatic major thirds (Czerny)

Czerny's fingering for chromatic thirds has been universally accepted. Chopin never wrote any major chromatic thirds in his compositions, and most likely for this reason was not interested in constructing a fingering.

Fingering for Chromatic Minor Thirds (Chopin)

Chopin used the first finger on consecutive white keys, (E-F), (B-C).
Liszt, among many others, liked to write major chromatic thirds.

31. Liszt: *Rhapsodie*, No. 15, Cadenza
Cadenza ad libitum

Well into the twentieth century, the rule existed to change fingers when repeating the same note several times. For the clavichord this rule was justified. If the player changed the finger when repeating the same key on the clavichord, it would create a peculiar vibrato *(Bebung)* as the string of the clavichord responded to modulation even after the finger had struck the key. Not so with the pianoforte. Once the hammer has hit the string you may just as well hold the key down with a broomstick.

Hans von Bülow, pianist and conductor, who had been Liszt's student and who became his son-in-law, adopted the rule of changing fingers which was accepted universally. Today we know better. If the student creates the desired effect without changing fingers, he should not abide by this outmoded rule.

32. Chopin: *Prelude*, Op. 28. No. 6

It is far easier to use the same finger, and the student will be well advised to use this method unless he needs very fast repetitions, as in some of Liszt's Hungarian Rhapsodies with their cimbalom imitations.

33. Liszt: *Rhapsodie hongroise*, No. 8

Occasionally we may find sustained or syncopated notes edited with a change of fingering. The student will find this very helpful, particularly for sustained notes.

34. Chopin: *Prelude*, Op. 28, No. 15
m. 1-3

chapter V

The correct way of using the pedal remains a study for life.

Frédéric Chopin

The Pedals

The pedal is the soul of the piano. With it we prolong resonance; without it, resonance dies quickly. Without sustaining the tone, the piano cannot sing. We can improve the tone through the use of the pedal, which helps to sustain the rapidly diminishing sound, yet the student will have to learn to master and use it discriminatingly.

A singer holds a tone through giving the proper support to his breathing, but that is just one single tone. When the pedal is down, all notes struck will be sustained until you lift your foot again and change it.

The ear is the best teacher. The beginner will soon learn to change pedal if the tones blur. The art of using it correctly and artistically has to be cultivated. Not every musician has the feel for it while for others it seems to come naturally. The student who studies a piece of music carefully for correct notes, best fingering and correct phrasing should be just as careful with the study of the pedals. It should not be left to impulse or used at random.

You must learn when to use the pedal and when to refrain from it. You need the help of the pedal for legato, to connect single tones and chords.

But when playing non-legato passages and when you want to create a clear effect, you must lift the pedal.

35. Mozart: *Sonata No. 8*, K. 311
m. 10-13

When changing the pedal, be sure not to raise the heel and lose contact with the pedal lever; then, instead of just pressing it down, you would be forced to step on it and create a disagreeable noise.

Very few composers gave exact pedal markings. Liszt, Chopin, Schumann and Brahms did write them into their music but were not very conscientious about it, nor did they always write the necessary changes.

Sonatas by Haydn and Clementi, and some by Mozart, can be played without the use of the pedal; however, with pedal they certainly sound better. To say that Mozart was against the use of the pedal is false.*

It is certainly any student's delight to play a beautiful legato without the use of the pedal. We need pedal also to create atmosphere and coloring, and it depends on the composer and style of composition whether the pedal should be used sparingly or not. For light texture, often in Schubert, we may change constantly during one harmony, although holding the pedal down would create no harmonic blur.

36. Schubert: *Impromptu,* Op. 90, No. 1, m. 41 -46

For full and rich or subdued atmosphere, often in Brahms and Debussy, one may decide against constant pedal change.

*See Chapter VI, p. 76, second paragraph.

37. Brahms: *Rhapsodie, Op. 79, No. 2, G minor*
m. 45-52

Molto passionato, ma non troppo allegro

There are innumerable possibilities for achieving effects which the intelligent student will discover for himself.

Students are often inclined to overlook the usefulness of the sostenuto pedal. Its purpose is to sustain single notes or specific chords, thus avoiding blurs the damper pedal would cause if held through various harmonies. It was invented in 1862 by Claude Montal and later perfected by Steinway. Although rarely indicated by composers as a pedal, modern composers have been utilizing it. It is indispensable for composers of the contemporary idiom, and its use for earlier works should not be ruled out. Faithful renditions and special effects, often attainable only with the sostenuto pedal, need careful attention and study.

38. Bach. J.S.: *The Well-Tempered Clavier, Book I, Fugue XX*
last measures

The left pedal, which we call the soft or *una corda* pedal, when depressed shifts the keyboard and hammers simultaneously to the right so that the hammer reaches two strings instead of three and, in sympathy, the untouched string vibrates feebly. At the time of Beethoven it was possible to shift farther so that the hammer might just contact one string, the player thus changing the tone coloring. There are several instances where Beethoven wrote *"due corde"* into his music, expecting the performer, with sensitive and careful use of the pedal, to shift to *una corda*.

Use the soft pedal sparingly, as for example when repeating indentical phrases and with the intention of changing the color. Try to get soft tones by hand and not by pedal.

The soft pedal is more effective in the treble than the bass. For composers such as Haydn and Mozart, you may want to limit the strength of your *forte* in consideration of the instruments of that period, and therefore you may want to use the soft pedal when playing *fortissimo*.

In general, the pedal should always be changed *after* the beat, *after* the chord. If you want an individual tone to be particularly beautiful, catch it with the pedal just after you have hit it. This is known as syncopated pedal. Your tone will stand out and sing. Schubert's *Impromptu*, Op. 90, No. 3 and Liszt's *Liebestraum* are recommended for pedal study.

39. Schubert: Impromptu, Op. 90, No. 3
m. 1 - 8

40. Liszt: Notturno III (Liebesträume)
m. 1 - 3

Another rule to follow: Pedal and hands should be lifted simultaneously, unless you intend to create a special effect. If it is done carelessly, it is bad.

Sight-reading

Not every student is a good sight-reader. There are gifted ones who can read almost anything you put before them; and strange as it may seem, good sight-readers may have a difficult time memorizing. Then again, those who memorize easily may have to go over the music note for note. For good sight-reading, one should begin when one is young.

Sight-reading should be a part of each lesson, provided there is sufficient time. Part of the preparation for the next lesson can be to read several pages or pieces. At the beginning, the student should take easy, short pieces, and as he acquires more self-assurance, he may tackle more difficult ones, more varied in style. He can repeat each piece two or three times and then go on to the next, as it is not important to play it perfectly. It is not my intention to encourage carelessness, but the objective remains: quick assimilation and playing rhythmically. Perfection comes later, and the student should not be discouraged if he does not always play the right notes. The more methodically he goes about his sight-reading sessions, the more perfect he will become. The brain will rely on the subconscious, and the eyes and fingers will, in time, learn to coordinate; with self-assurance, good timing will also be acquired.

Once sight-reading becomes routine, the student should get thoroughly acquainted with contemporary composers. Shostakovich's *Twenty-four Preludes,* Opus 34, and Kabalevsky's, *Preludes* Opus 38, are good training for eyes and fingers. Shostakovich's *Prelude* No. 4 and Kabalevsky's Nos. 1 and 2 are easy reading.

41. Shostakovich: *Prelude,* Op. 34, No. 4
m. 1 - 9

42. Kabalevsky: *Prelude,* Op. 38, No. 1
m. 1 - 11

43. Kabalevsky: *Prelude,* Op. 38, No. 2
m. 1 - 14

Then one may proceed to more difficult ones. Bartók's and Prokofieff's works for the piano also have a great deal to offer and should not be neglected.

Duet playing, with the performers exchanging Primo and Secondo parts, is good schooling. It is not necessary to play slower than the power of concentration demands. Piano literature is rich in pieces for four hands. Diabelli is standard for beginners. Advanced students should tackle Schubert with his brisk tempo. Chamber music should also be cultivated.

The student who trains himself for sight-reading will soon discover that his eyes will wander ahead of the measure he is playing, and gradually, with alertness of mind, he will learn to think ahead of the sounds he is producing.

Omit no opportunity, however, to play with others in Duos, Trios, etc. It makes your playing fluent, spirited, and easy. Accompany a singer when you can.

Robert Schumann
Rules for Young Musicians

Memorizing

Memorizing is a necessity, and the magic word is concentration. In gaining confidence, not letting thoughts wander and listening attentively to one's own playing will help to absorb and retain the notes. When playing from memory, the student will gain self-assurance, the art of expression will come more naturally and he will learn that it is easier to play "by heart" than with the music in front of him. If the student memorizes correctly from the start, there will be fewer technical difficulties.

The easiest correct fingering must first be established. Going from note to note, phrase to phrase, and harmony to harmony will also train the student not to let the mind wander away from the notes. Naming the notes out loud and practicing from hand position to hand position can also be of help. How much a student can absorb at a time is individual. Concentration will also demand training. Certainly, the moment one tires, he should stop. After being refreshed and having regained control over one's mind, continue. Memorizing, even reading and visualizing away from the instrument, is good schooling as well since it helps to absorb the tonal and keyboard picture.

Anyone with a good memory or a photographic mind is blessed. A student who can memorize by playing a piece should, most certainly, do it that way; but special care should be taken not to become careless, to keep control of the conscious mind and never permit the subconscious to gain the upper hand. The time to beware of the subconscious is after one has mastered a piece and the fingers can find their places mechanically.

It is good practice to repeat memorized pieces from time to time with the music in front of you. Constantly working on one's memory by learning new music is bound to strengthen it, particularly if one plays attentively with a critical ear, listening to each tone, watching the fingering carefully, and absorbing the musical picture. Lack of practice may undermine ability. A part of daily practicing should include specific time for sight-reading and for memorizing.

It is our conscious mind that works when we play from memory. When reading, our brain relies on the subconscious.

Embellishments

What was the purpose of embellishments and why were they written? The answer is very simple. As early keyboard instruments were poor in tone intensity and could not sustain sound, the composer liked to beautify and ornament his compositions with embellishments to disguise this shortcoming. There was an unending variety of them which the player had to know, although he did not always observe them, nor was he required to observe them strictly. He also improvised to his heart's content in the Baroque era (ca. 1550-1750), in which the ornate and the highly elaborate were considered in good taste. With the appearance of the pedal, the embellishments had outlived their purpose and gradually disappeared.

The student does not have to make a study of embellishments, as most piano editions have explanatory footnotes or show the embellishments written out, if not specified in the preface. Before Beethoven and Hummel, long and short grace notes had to be played *with* the bass note, on the beat.

44. Scarlatti, D.: *Sonata, K. 308,* C major
m. 27

to be played

In music after that period they are played *before* the beat. Bach often wrote out embellishments, as in the slow movement of the *Italian Concerto.*

45. Bach, J.S.: Italian Concerto, Second movement
m. 12

46. Ibid.
m. 28

Compare measure 28 with measure 35.

m. 35

compare with

With the Mannheim School (ca. 1725-1790), fancy embellishments were on their way out. Haydn, Mozart and Schubert made little use of them. Beethoven turned against them, and long and short grace notes, mordents and turns were used sparingly. Chopin still made extensive use of embellishments, but his style of writing them is clear and there should be no doubt as to how to play them.

47. Chopin: *Nocturne*, Op. 32, No. 1
m. 28 - 30

Schumann, Mendelssohn, Brahms and their contemporaries practically forgot about them.

Octaves

Liszt was once asked by one of his pupils, August Stradal, how to practice octaves, and gave the answer, "Don't practice them. Play them." However, the student cannot just sit down and play octaves. Here the time element and endurance training are involved since the muscles used for octaves are not in constant use. To play Liszt's *Rhapsody* No. 6, for example, with its pages of octaves, is no simple undertaking. These demands can be made of an accomplished pianist who may have spent years of study to reach perfection. To apply the same standards to a student would be folly. Your common sense must tell you that this demands endurance training for the muscles. You do not go on a ten-hour hike without conditioning yourself and preparing for it gradually.

One can easily ruin the hands with tension and by overworking muscles. Technique develops gradually, and the ability to play thundering or pianissimo octaves cannot be mastered overnight.

Hofmann and Godowsky played octaves in a legato-like manner. Others play them with a stiff wrist or a swinging wrist; the latter is not the easiest way. Vladimir Horowitz captures his audience by playing his octaves with vibration of the entire arm.

Speed and endurance can be acquired through steady practice. Practice octaves in scales, in broken chords, in any fashion that strikes your fancy. But be methodical, and do not jump from one exercise to the other. Practice them like any other exercise: legato, staccato, slow, fast, pianissimo and fortissimo. Keep a light wrist and avoid stiffness in the muscles and in the forearm. *Rest the arm as soon as you get tired.*

Staccato movement is a natural fundamental motion for playing octaves. The thumb, which can not be substituted for any other finger, skips from tone to tone, and if we want to create the illusion of legato, we can only do so by using (3rd), 4th and 5th fingers alternately.

When playing octaves chromatically the wrist may naturally and easily move up and down as well as laterally.

For fast octaves we hold the wrist passive, and the moving vehicle is the forearm. When playing octaves staccato, use the first and fifth fingers on both black and white keys.

48. Brahms: *Sonata*, Op. 2, F♯ minor
m. 1 - 2

The first two measures, combining arpeggio chords with fortissimo octaves, are not overtaxing and can be turned into a study by repeating five to ten times.

49. Ibid.
m. 7-8

Measures 7-8 can also be treated as a study.

Works that challenge octave playing are Czerny's *Six Octave Studies*, Op. 553. The student will be well advised not to miss them.

50. Czerny: *Six Octave Studies*, **Op. 553**
Study No. 1, m. 1 - 2

m. 9 - 10

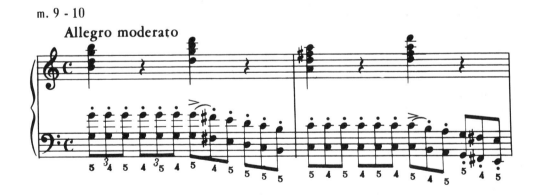

No. 2, m. 1-2

Allegro comodo

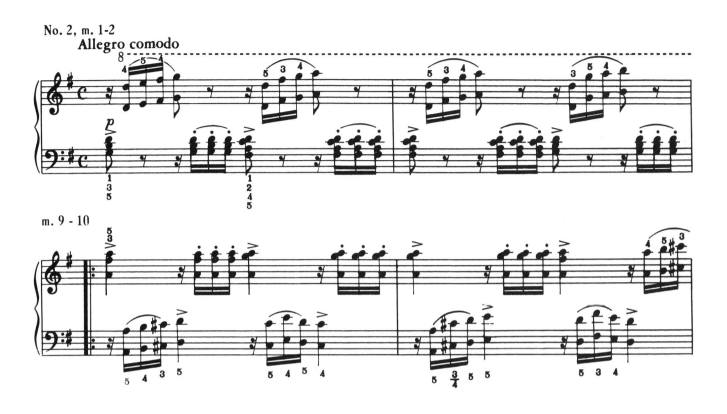

m. 9 - 10

No. 3, m. 1 - 3

Allegro scherzando

m. 17 - 19

No. 4, m. 1 - 2

Molto allegro

m. 9 - 10

No. 5, m. 1 - 2

Molto vivace

m. 9 - 10

m. 17 - 18

No. 6, m. 1 - 2

Allegro vivo, con bravura

Czerny's melodious *Octave Study,* Op. 740, Book 5, makes demands on the accomplished pianist. A student will gain by working on this study several bars at a time from memory in a slower tempo than called for.

51. Czerny: Octave Study, Op. 740, Book 5
m. 1-4   **Molto allegro** ♩. = 112

Octave skips, the hand light.

52. Chopin: Etude, Op. 25, No. 10
m. 1-3   **Allegro con fuoco** ♩ = 72

chapter VI

Phrasing and Style

The inside of the piano has the shape of a harp. The harpist plucks the strings with his fingers to produce tone from the instrument, but the pianist has not this possibility. He needs an intermediary, the key, to produce a tone. The forte, the pianissimo, the crescendo, the diminuendo, in short, all the different shadings, are the colorings that bring music to life, without which it could not hold the attention of the listener.

Each generation has a different concept of music and how it should be performed. Composers mirror their times. The eighteenth century could not have created a Stravinsky, nor could the twentieth century have created a Mozart. How should one present music written several centuries ago for instruments with small sound volume? In the era of Bach, Haydn, and Mozart, composers never dreamed of grand pianos with such tremendous sound volume as those in our day. Why not try to bring compositions of this period to their full beauty by taking advantage of the tone and sound possibilities of today's instruments — *without abuse to the style of the period.*

Much confusion and controversy can be avoided if composers will not neglect editing, if they will treat it as part of the composition. We are grateful if we do not have to decide on phrasing; we prefer the composer's own editing. But if the composer has not painstakingly edited his work to the last detail, there can be more than one solution to a phrasing problem.

I wish to make the student conscious of well-edited piano literature, as all is not necessarily well that looks well. Without question, the inexperienced student will not discriminate but will accept any edition of a work he intends to study. Only experience and gradually acquired knowledge will guide him to compare editions so as to make his own decision.

Bach contributed to the confusion. As was customary at the time, he wrote no tempi, no dynamics; he never indicated if the performer was to play legato or leggiero; and, as he often wrote one and the same piece for the violin and harpsichord, we cannot be too far wrong in believing that he did not care on what medium it would be produced.

Will the editor, the link between composer and performer, who is attempting this big task, know where to indicate legato, where to write ties, where to add, change and phrase? Will he know if phrasing was omitted intentionally, or if it was omitted with the purpose of giving the performer an opportunity to prove his own taste? Only if the editor, the scholar, understands the style and feels the pulse of the composition, only then can he do the composer justice.

Whenever an editor leaves the original untouched and indicates his phrasing and revisions separately, as ossias, it gives the performer confidence that he is dealing with one whose foremost thought is the preservation of the composer's intent.

What is a phrase? Can we compare a phrase in music to a sentence in speech? We cannot. One single sentence, with so many words, can express one complete thought. It need not necessarily lead to more sentences. One musical phrase, a cohesive musical idea consisting of several bars, must lead to one or more phrases to be complete. We talk, we breathe, we observe punctuation marks, we change the pitch of our voices, and thus express and convey a thought. In music, the composer expresses a thought in connected tones; he brings to life a melody which the student or the accomplished pianist tries to grasp and bring to life in his own way.

To bring music to life demands more than just production of successions of sounds. The sense of continuity leads from one release to the other, or to a climax as in the ending of a piece. The music in its flow goes somewhere; it has to convey something. It releases emotions in the listener while *the performer's emotions are kept under control.* The pianist, the true artist, must compromise, as he may not let his personality dominate. The student must also try to bring a composition to life, acquiring his own style, not trying to imitate other artists. He will be guided by phrasing notations which he should observe carefully.

It is quite impossible to construct laws for phrasing. One should compare phraseology in music to syntax in language.

Slurs and Legato

The student must become acquainted with phrasing marks step by step, and when studying a piece of music, not be negligent in observing them. If he sees a slur over several bars, he knows the composer indicated legato playing.

53. Brahms: *Intermezzo,* Op. 76. No. 6, A major
m. 25 - 27

If a slur connects two notes or chords, then the first note must be more pronounced than the second; and as we have learned to give accents, this is a good opportunity to stress the first note. It gives a highlight, provides the nuance the composer intended.

54. Chopin: *Ballade* No. 3, Op. 47, A♭
m. 9-11

Legato means playing smoothly, in a flowing manner. An even and smooth legato can be achieved if the fingers are not unduly raised, but held close to the keyboard. The notes or chords have to be bound together either by pedal or skillful fingering; the notes must not overlap and the melodic line must not become blurred. There is only one legato; it is impossible to be more or less legato. We either bind notes together or we do not. It should be any student's delight to play a beautiful smooth legato without the help of the pedal.

A master in this art is Vladimir Horowitz. I have watched Horowitz's use of the pedals very carefully. For example, in Chopin's Nocturne, Opus 15, No. 2, bars 6, 7, and 8, he produces an impeccable legato. No pedal; instead, he uses only the soft pedal, which creates a very special effect.

Larghetto

Legatissimo

Legatissimo (very smoothly) is used for passages or figurations that are purely decorative, such as those in Debussy, Ravel and Chopin. In this case, the "slappy" touch — like a person too lazy to open his mouth properly when talking — will create the atmosphere desired.

Relaxed wrist and forearm. Unrestricted elbow joint.

56. Chopin: *Berceuse*
m. 41

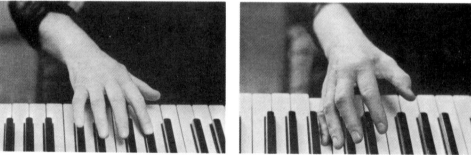

Leggiero (in a light manner)

Non-legato playing will always add an element of color. It is very helpful to raise the fingers, and good effects are also produced when playing with the tips of the fingers, even "throwing" the fingers. All of these variations will produce different nuances.

Ritardando

Ritardando is a gradual slackening of tempo at the end of a phrase. If written in the middle of a composition, the original tempo should be resumed at the indication "a tempo."

Rubato

Rubato, rarely written into the music and often incorrectly used as ritardando, has an element of syncopation. A note, or notes, are momentarily robbed of length, while the accompanying figuration observes a strict tempo. Mozart's rubato, as well as Chopin's, required a rigorous perception of tempo. We can find rubato written into some of Mozart's music and in these rare instances, there can be no doubt in the performer's mind as to its execution. If not written into the music, this must be left to the student's or performer's taste. Although it is not imperative, without question it is more correct if the tempo is resumed.

Chopin considered rubato, as well as ritardando, very important for expressive playing, and also believed that any changes in tempo demanded compensation. Acceleration should follow ritardando, and vice versa, so that the long phrases should all have the same length in time, which in most cases is controlled by the bass notes. With freedom of the right hand, the left hand should play in strict tempo. This is the explanation of the old Mozart rule, *im Takt spielen* (playing in rhythm). Chopin, when expressing himself on tempo rubato, made the very poetic comparison with a tree where the leaves move while the trunk remains immobile. Tempo rubato, when not out of control or used with too much liberty, will be of great interpretive value to the student.

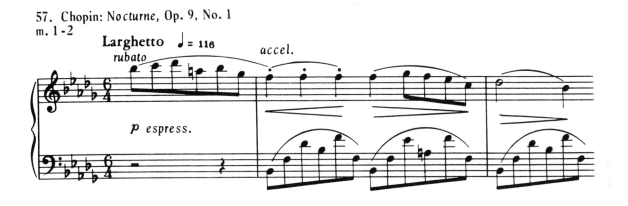

Music should never be played metronomically, as it would be robbed of all beauty of expression. If you compare jazz music, where metronomic playing is imperative, to classical music, the value of the point I have just made will be fully understood. The Metronome has the purpose only of checking tempi; the student should not practice with it. It will kill expression. When in doubt as to what tempo to take if the metronome marking is not correctly indicated, the wise words of Mozart's father Leopold in his *Violinschule** (Violin School) can be a student's guide. "Every melodious piece has at least one phrase from which one can recognize quite surely what sort of speed the piece demands."

Chopin was just as strict in demanding dynamic changes as he was with his tempi; he expected different shading for each repeat of a phrase or short motif; Scarlatti as well as his contemporaries demanded that repetitions of phrases be played differently each time. Turk's rules for changing shading in repetitions, either making an echo effect or reversing the dynamics, are still in effect today.

---

*Blom, Eric. *Mozart's Letters.* Translated and annotated by Emily Anderson.

58. Scarlatti, D.: *Sonata, K. 517, D minor*
m. 25-32

Prestissimo

A student must not phrase at random, and he must know that he has to *reach the key bed with every tone he strikes*. He should learn to master tone shading from triple piano to triple forte.

If a melody has to be brought out, keep the accompanying figuration softer, and the melody will sing. The easiest way to accomplish this is to play the tones which carry the melody with the weight of your arm. If one hand carries melody and accompaniment, treat it the same way. (See Excerpts 39 and 40.)

When playing different rhythms with each hand, attention should be focused on the hand that carries the theme, the melody, as then the accompaniment will flow along smoothly, as in the Fantaisie-Impromptu, Op. 66, by Chopin.

59. Chopin: *Fantaisie-Impromptu*, Op. 66
m. 1 - 8

Starting with measure 5, it may be left to the student's taste whether or not he wishes to change the pedal twice in each bar. The right hand plays 8/16 against 6/8 in the left hand. First get the right hand with the melody in good order, and the left hand will take care of itself. Trying to play both hands equally strong when playing different rhythms is not advisable, as both hands will sound equally loud, and accompaniment will kill the melody.

For Chopin's F minor Etude No. 1 (no opus) the same rule applies as in the preceding example. Practicing slowly and giving accents on first and third beat, or one in each bar, will facilitate mastering this etude. Once order has been established, the student will gradually arrive at the correct tempo, ♩=ca. 72, the accents will disappear, and one can concentrate on progression, build-up, and tone shading.

60. Chopin: *Etude No. 1,* F minor (without opus number)
m. 1 - 21 **Andantino**

For the next example, attention is focused on the accents Scriabin has written for the left hand. In this Prelude, practice *bar for bar,* with light wrists, carefully observing the accents, in a slower tempo than indicated. Practicing each figure individually is perfectly in order. Also, preparing for the different hand positions is advisable.

61. Scriabin: *Prelude, Op. 13, No. 4*
m. 1 - 8

A student who builds up a piece to the climax, a fortissimo, must evaluate his timing, his power and his strength. Say to yourself that there is plenty of time, as the more deliberately you go about it the more effective it will be. Power has limitations. Do not let your temperament run away with you, or you will waste power. Do not let your emotions get the best of you.

If a student wants to fully understand composers, he should read their biographies and letters, as with this knowledge and insight, the study of a composition at the piano will be more intelligible.

Summary of Various Composers' Styles and Approach to Studying Their Works

In the study of Bach, who is a demanding master, the student must focus his utmost attention on correct reading. Within the confines of strict rules, this greatest of all craftsmen could unlock depths, pour out and express his deepest emotions and attain heights of unequaled grandeur and beauty. With methodical workout, the correct value of notes and rests can be strictly observed, so that the release of each individual hand will be precise. If carelessly practiced the hands may be released too soon or too late, which in either case diverges from the Bach style. We do not build up gradual crescendo or decrescendo. In the main, dynamics change abruptly from one level to another level.

The use of the weight of arm method, holding the hand quiet and playing a smooth and even legato, will be of greatest interpretive value. When playing two- to four-voiced fugues, where we hold and move in one hand, the quiet hand is imperative. In the study of Bach, the student will find the soundest approach to acquiring a well-rounded technique; if he plays Bach in the early stages of his studies, it will open the doors for him to other composers.

Bach was no pioneer; his style was not influenced by any past or contemporary century. He was completion and fulfillment in itself, like a meteor which follows its own path, his greatness hardly recognized until almost a century after his passing.

> Practice industriously the fugues of good masters, above all those of Johann Sebastian Bach. Make the *Well-tempered Clavier* your daily bread; then you will surely be a thorough musician.
>
> Robert Schumann
> *Rules for Young Musicians*

Mozart, who was considered the first pianoforte virtuoso, was a born pianist who played with a great deal of expression, and who was proud of his "beautiful pure tone." His music indicates that his playing must have been governed by strict simplicity. He wrote with good balance and in classic style. Brightness, gaiety, grace, crisp sparkle and sparkling strength, as well as sorrow, are the components to look for in Mozart's music. When studying Mozart, strict rhythm should be observed, and to comply with the texture of his music, I suggest that the student lift the fingers (more than when playing Beethoven), to play more from the wrist than from the arm, and to play more with the tips of the fingers than the cushions. Use non-legato playing unless otherwise indicated by slurs; passages should be clear and sparkling, and the pedal should be sparingly and discriminately used. Mozart himself never intended that his works should be played completely without the use of pedal.

A composer may have painstakingly edited his work, yet he cannot possibly write all the terms necessary for minor interpretation into the music. As stated, knowledge of style for the individual composers should be acquired by the student. With concentrated study of a composition, after the technical aspects have been mastered, the finer points of execution and the right proportions for the tempo will come naturally.

> Only when the form is entirely clear to you, will the spirit become clear.
>
> Robert Schumann
> *Rules for Young Musicians*

It is easy to learn the sense of form from Beethoven, easier than from Bach, since Beethoven's melodies develop into large ideas which usually contain several figures.

The student has familiarized himself with the weight-of-arm method, and Beethoven is a composer with whom this method can be most appropriately utilized. Visualize Beethoven with his square shoulders and beautiful head of thick, unruly hair. Absorb this mental picture, and then put your fingers on the keys. The feeling for Beethoven, whose noble grandeur has never been equalled, will come to you effortlessly. You will hold your fingers curved, more so than when playing Chopin, but instead of thinking of the fingers, you will become conscious of the arms, particularly the forearms. Although the fingers will have to do the work, the arm will be the power behind the hand.

In Beethoven we look for impassioned energy, rich harmonies, full tones, harmonious legato and humor. "Rondo a capriccio" in G major, also known under the title "Rage over a lost penny," is proof of my last statement.

Liberal, strictly disciplined use of the pedal is perfectly in order. If the student wants to test his own ability and convince himself of the technical and musical differences between Mozart and Beethoven, he may play a Mozart sonata in the Beethoven manner, or vice versa. This will speak better than words.

A well-educated music student will recognize the composer on the written page through his style of writing. After years of study, it would be impossible for him to mistake a page of Beethoven for Bach, Mozart, Chopin, Brahms or any other composer.

62. Schubert: *Impromptu, Op. 90, No. 4*

m. 1 - 2

As an example, take Schubert's Impromptu No. 4, Op. 90.

In the first bars, Schubert established the rhythm, which must be observed throughout. There is no change in tempo; it is all one pattern. In the right hand's sixteenth-notes, where any ritardando would be out of place, the style of writing lays down the law in itself. The demanded effects will be obtained with skillful dynamics and skillful use of the pedals. As mentioned in the chapter on the pedals, you may get a ritardando effect through lifting the pedal, as it breaks the tones; you "cheat" your audience, but you get the effect you desire while remaining true to the style required. To maintain the true Schubert texture, the student will find a constant pedal change very helpful, even if no dissonance were created in holding it.

63. Ibid. Trio

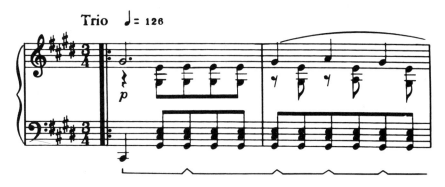

In the Trio, which may be played a bit slower, where the right hand carries the melody and accompaniment, the tempo may not change. However, here you can also create a very impressive effect with skillful use of the pedal. I suggest catching the G-sharp (the first note in the right hand) with the pedal. Linger a second or so, and change the pedal again on the second beat, holding it until the first beat of the next bar. Here you make three pedal changes, taking special care to bring out the top notes. This will sound beautiful, and you will not have committed the offense of bringing ritardando into Schubert's music. If you play the Trio like Schumann, with lingering melodies and ritardando, you will divert from the true Schubert style.

Schubert was on the threshold of the romantic style. He was poetic but not sentimental. There are no lingering melodies as in Schumann, the true romantic.

Brahms, the classic romanticist, is often referred to as the successor of Beethoven. To Brahms, the great purist, one can surely apply Schumann's dictum: "Mastery of form leads talent to ever-increasing freedom." His classical form which reached supreme heights, forever striving for perfection, was void of all superficial tonal effects.

There is no need for any pedagogue to come forward with suggestions as to round fingers, curved fingers, or what not. Any student who masters dynamics and tone shadings from triple piano to triple forte will love Brahms, with his ever-changing moods, and will do well in studying him. The tempi are flexible, broadening, then stepping up again; and the great scope in dynamics gives many possibilities. Brahms' full texture and sweep permits free and liberal use of the pedal. (See Excerpt No. 37.)

When the student turns to the impressionists, the approach should be just as thorough, although other demands are made on the performer. Debussy abandoned emotionalism, large forms, and climaxes, and with this new style came atmosphere and color, the outstanding Debussy characteristics. To create the Debussy atmosphere and color, we apply the "slappy" touch, as was discussed in the chapter on tone and touch. Let your curved fingers fall on the keys; the impact of the fingers on the keys is on the cushions, as far back from the tips as possible. There are tricks to every trade. If the student can get the desired effect with the tips of his fingers, he should stick to his guns. But whatever is done should not be done cn a moment's impulse. Careful pedal study should be observed and the running passages be made supple, with shading. This adds color to a Debussy composition.

It is the student's duty to observe conscientiously each composer's specific style and form, for stylistic execution is no less important than correct execution of notes, tempi and phrasing.

chapter VII

TEACHING BEGINNERS

One can teach any child to play the piano beyond the preliminary stages. Certainly, a grownup can be taught the instrument, but it is easier to learn when young, with a growing hand. For the grownup there will always be technical difficulties. With the child, we will soon find out if he is talented, if he is musical, has good coordination or even an innate aptitude for technique.

Whatever method or system the individual teacher uses for teaching, when being guided by his own ideas, he should avoid mental blindness. There is no one way.

Instructions should be as uncomplicated as possible. *Give, do not take* should be the main principle for a good instructor. Do not overtax the beginner. The simpler the better. As in good writing, omit unnecessary words.

The beginner's book should not be cluttered up with too many instructions. The student, no matter what his age, will become flustered, and the teacher will have difficulty in holding his attention. One should draw the student's attention to the fact that an individual tone is not music but connected tones are. Students soon learn to observe slurs, to connect tones, so that there is a continuation of sound. Phrasing and making pleasing music shall go hand in hand with correct reading. The teacher should estimate how much a student can absorb and then make sure that he has absorbed the entire lesson.

It is very common to speak of the fingers "hitting" or "striking" the keys. For beginners, "depressing" is more an appropriate term; the fingers should fall on the keys. Let the student listen to the tone. Explain that the hammer hits the string, producing the sound, the tone, and then falls back immediately. After the key has once been depressed, the player has no more influence over the sound that has been produced.

After you have told the student to let the fingers fall on the keys, if he is not completely relaxed, tap slightly on the wrist. This is important with some students, as it will help to overcome any tension that may have set in. Should a tendency to raise the wrist persist, try temporarily seating him with the elbows slightly below keyboard level. Often simply being overanxious to do everything right may cause the tension.

The teacher should make it easy for the student, introducing new things step by step and making very sure that he is thoroughly familiar with all he has been taught so far. Only then introduce something new. Leave nothing hanging in mid-air. With group teaching this pattern can also be followed; however, the pace is bound to be slower than with individual instruction.

At the very first lesson familiarize the student with the keyboard and the written notes simultaneously. At this stage, do not be concerned with the seating position. The student, particularly a child, may prefer standing in front of the piano to look for the keys. Show him that there are two black keys and then three black keys, and that this pattern repeats itself. Let him look for the black keys over the entire keyboard. For the black keys we need our longest and strongest fingers. 2, 3, and 4. With each hand separately, let him depress these keys over the entire keyboard: right hand 2-3, 2-3-4; left hand 2-3-4, 2-3.

To the left of the two central black keys, we find the note "C". Let him look for all the C's over the entire keyboard. Then proceed to D, which lies between the two black keys, and then on to E, which is just to the right of the two black keys. He can now have his fun looking for all the duplications of the three notes he has learned.

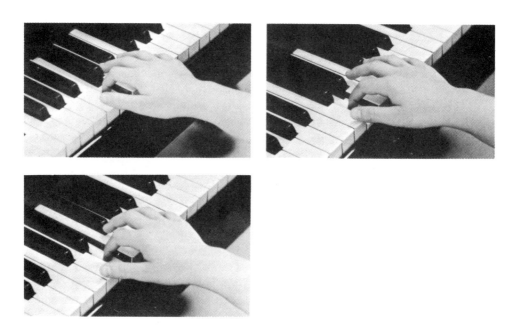

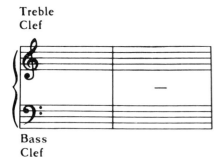

Stop right there and do not continue to look for further notes.

The accompanying diagram shows two staves with five lines each, which belong together. Notes are written on and between the lines. This is one measure with the treble clef sign and the bass clef sign. For the middle C we draw an extra line in between the two staffs.

Treble Clef

Bass Clef

The student learns that he can make use of the center line, the C, for both the right hand and the left hand. If we need it for the treble clef, we place it higher, and if we need it for the bass clef, we place it lower.

The C divides the treble clef from the bass clef.

Then we show the student the C an octave higher and an octave lower, but without mentioning the word "octave." In the right hand (treble clef) the C is just *above* the middle staff line, and in the left hand (bass clef) just *below* the middle staff line. If he is anxious to know where he can find the next C's, we can draw it on the board or the music sheet, two lines above and two lines below the staff lines. Although we will not make use of all these C's in the near future, it is quite entertaining for the student to know where he can find them on the written page and on the piano.

So far, the teacher has focused the student's attention only on the keyboard and the written notes, without correcting the seating or the hand position. Now we come to the next phase, which is just as important for group teaching as for individual instruction. MAKE SURE THAT THE STUDENT HAS THE CORRECT POSITION AT THE KEYBOARD. (See Chapter I, pp. 1-3.)

With these correct hand and seating positions, the student now places both thumbs on middle C. Like a fruit that ripens outward from the center, so we add note after note and tone after tone from middle C. Begin there and spread in both directions, teaching treble and bass from the start. Make it easy for the student, and place his fingers right where they belong.

Since the student has learned three notes, C, D, E, he can play them with his right hand. With the left hand, pick up the two connecting notes, B and A. The student should have his hands in the right position and begin with the music in front of him. Assist the student and lift his hand at rests.

In $\frac{4}{4}$ time we count 4 beats to the measure and the whole note is held for 4 beats.

Whole note   Whole rest

As notes are written on the lines and on spaces between the lines, and as the student's hands are placed in proper position, he will quickly read and play the following example.

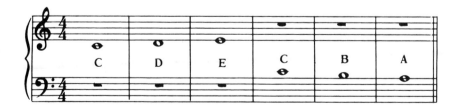

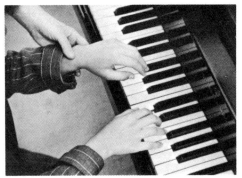

The student can now read and play five notes.

He should name the notes while he is playing them, C-D-E, C-B-A. Repeat this several times. Then have him count four while he is playing; it is not a bad idea to let him play and count in the following manner:

C,2,3,4
D,2,3,4
E,2,3,4 etc.

After this example, turn to the next ones, which are also exercises in counting and naming the notes.

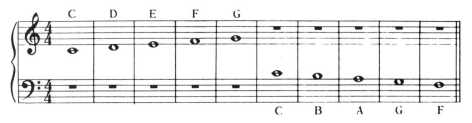

He can now read and play five notes with the right hand, and five notes with the left hand. We have established a starting point and can now gradually add additional notes.

At his first lesson he has learned to read and play nine notes. Starting with middle C, he can play with all five fingers from C to G in the right hand and from C to F in the left hand. The five-finger position is basic for all piano playing.

The student has learned to sit correctly at the piano.
He has learned how to place his hands correctly on the keys.
He has learned the treble clef.
He has learned the bass clef.
He has learned the value of a whole-note.
He has learned the value of a whole-rest.

A simple system from which to branch out has thus been established and through continuing in this pattern, the student will learn to read and play simultaneously with both hands. When playing, the student should name the notes, beginning with the left hand. Thus he learns to read correctly from the start. We introduce half-notes, half-rests, quarter-notes, and quarter-rests as we go along. All this the student will pick up without the least effort. It will make his lessons enjoyable and capture his interest. Hard work will set in soon enough, since the instructor cannot do the practicing for the student; but he learns the fundamentals in this easy way. He learns the notes as he learned the letters of the alphabet, and if he should discover that the piano holds his interest (the student may be gifted and learn to love the instrument), then the instructor has helped him on the right road.

As we pick up more and more notes, the hand will not remain over the same keys. We will move the hand at the beginning, over connecting notes; for the right hand we want the fingers over the keys D to A, then E to B, or the left hand over B to E, etc. We do this because a student should not identify a key with a finger.

As soon as this has been absorbed, we progress and go into a little talk on the thumb, who is now the "good boy" and not (as in the chapter on the thumb) the culprit. Be as concise as possible. Tell the student that since the thumb, unlike the other fingers, has the ability to move sideways to depress a key, we shall certainly take advantage of this. We have no intention of disturbing the peaceful coexistence between the 2nd, 3rd, 4th, and 5th fingers.

There is no further danger that the student will identify the individual fingers with specific keys or notes; we advance to the next step. The student will learn to make the proper use of the thumb, and the instructor can make up some exercises. For example:

The student now knows that the thumb is independent and that the space between the second finger and the thumb can be enlarged at will.

We have learned the stretch and can now turn to the passing of the thumb under the hand.

One can not teach a beginner a fast motion, particularly not the fast disappearing of the thumb under the hand. As the brain gives the command for the execution, we must admit that this order is unusual and unfamiliar. With the principle in mind of making things as easy as possible, we again place both thumbs on the middle C. He will now play 1-2, 1-2, several times as we make it clear to him that, when the second fingers come down, the thumbs must move under the hand at the same time. IT HAS TO BE ONE MOTION. We do not want to see the thumbs.

Then we continue 1-2-3, 1-2-3-4-5, and back to the middle C. This the student will play several times, but we *must watch* that the elbows do not move up into the air. With the motion of the thumb he may move his wrist slightly sideways so as to avoid strain, and with this motion the arm will move along, away from or closer to the body.

Since we intend to familiarize the student with scales in the beginning stages, we ask him: "Have you ever heard of the C major scale? Well, that's what you have been playing now. Now, let's have fun, and continue what you are playing to the next C." We let him play the C major scale with both hands in contrary motion.

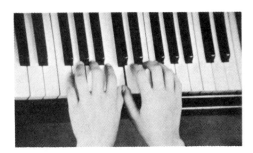
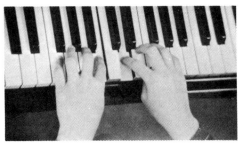

The student will soon learn to play little pieces, and, in going over them measure by measure, point out that there are always repeated notes and that by keeping his hand close to the keys, and in position, he will avoid having to look anew for the key he has just played. This goes for beginning and advanced students alike. Looking for hold-overs, for connections, for combinations, he quickly learns to look ahead of the notes he is playing if taught to do so in the beginning stages. *He learns to read correctly.*

The instructor should work out the most advantageous fingering; even if there is fingering printed in the music, as it usually is, he should not hesitate to make changes. With beginners, avoid using the thumb on black keys before they are thoroughly familiar with the keyboard. As soon as a student can play without looking at his hands, we will no longer consider him a beginner. This is the first sign of self-assurance.

In what beginner's books will the instructor find everything to his liking? You will, of course, choose books you consider superior, but in spite of that, you may want to make changes, alter fingering, skip or rearrange the order of pieces. Do so. It is not essential to go through a book in sequential fashion.

A student can never be taught too early to listen attentively to his own playing, to the sounds he is producing. He must become sound-conscious and know that tones and notes must be connected unless otherwise indicated by notation. In the whole study of music, ear training and constant listening must be considered of paramount importance.

In the first months of training the instructor may draw the student's attention to sound just by asking, "Did you like the way this sounded?" This does not necessitate a lecture on tone production. It is so much simpler, as long as a student's fingers are not as yet entirely at his command, to say: "Let's give a slight accent on this or that note," or "Give an accent on the first of each beat." Or "This note is not important, as it is the introduction. The next note is." One might also say, "Now let's build this entire phrase up to the last measure."

The instructor who possesses creative instructive ability will think for himself and not just follow pedagogical grooves. There is no one supreme method. Experience will guide him as to what course to follow.

Students will gradually learn the correct terminology. One of the first words that will mean something to him is the word legato. Then comes piano (soft), forte (loud), crescendo (getting louder), decrescendo (getting softer). The word "staccato" may be an exciting one to learn.

I like to present each of my students with a pocket-sized dictionary of musical terms; it helps them to expand their knowledge of the language and terms in music.

The Scales

The student has learned to play C major with hands in contrary motion, and the correct finger pattern for the scales has been established. He can make use of the entire keyboard without any difficulties. Before we turn to a new scale, the student should first learn to play C major *individually*. We start with the right hand, the first finger on middle C, and play over three or four octaves several times. The left hand gets the same treatment, but, starting with the 5th finger one or two octaves lower. This is more difficult than playing both hands together in contrary motion. 1-2-3, 1-2-3-4, 1-2-3, etc., was an entertaining, undemanding game by comparison.

The next step the instructor has to "play by ear," since it is impossible to lay down an absolute law and insist that the student play the scales in parallel motion within the first two months. If the student is old enough and grasps things easily, there should be no unnecessary delay in letting him start to play both hands together in parallel motion as soon as possible.

Then we continue to teach in proper order the next four scales, G, D, A and E major. As we are dealing with beginners, we shall teach the development of scales the primitive, easy way. (More mature students should be taught the theoretical development of scales right from the start: two whole-steps, one half-step, three whole-steps and one half-step.)

The student can already play C major; now he has to find the next scale. All we do is move the student's hand up five keys and arrive at the note G. G major is the scale that follows C major. As we develop major scales by one pattern, we shall always raise the 7th degree (7th note) a half-step; thus we add new sharps as we go along, one new one for each new scale. In G major, the seventh tone, the F, will be raised a half-step to F-sharp.

With the thumb on G, and with the right hand, we start our pattern: 1-2-3 and 1-2-3-4-5. In this fashion we introduce him to the first black key, the first sharp. He shall now play G major with the right hand, naming the notes as he plays them, then repeating the pattern over three to four octaves. He should think from G to G, from octave to octave.

As we let the student look for the next three scales, D, A, and E major (always moving up five keys), the instructor should make the following quite clear. THE SHARPS WHICH WE HAVE ADDED FOR EACH NEW SCALE ARE THERE TO STAY.

There are fifteen major scales, all constructed alike. Over a very short period the student will learn to play a group of five scales, C,G,D,A and E major, the last of which, E major, has four sharps.

For B, F#, and C# major, the new group with all the black keys, we must look for a new approach. The student will play B major, adding the new sharp, the A-sharp, and again naming the keys. (When we let him name the sharps separately, it is always in their proper succession, F#, C#, G#, D#, A#, etc.; regular quiz sessions are advisable.) Since we need all the black keys for these last three scales, we play them with the long fingers as we were taught at the first lesson, 2-3, 2-3-4. We repeat our previous instruction, and let the student depress the black keys simultaneously in this order over several octaves, so that there is no doubt in the student's mind as to what fingers to use for the following three scales.

Since we know the notes for B major, we shall now get the thumb into action and play in the following manner:

Thumb on B, depress 2 black keys simultaneously.

Thumb on E, depress 3 black keys simultaneously.

Do this several times over the entire keyboard, the left hand using the same procedure but in the opposite direction, so that three black keys are depressed first. Take each hand separately. This is very entertaining for the student and he has learned to play the B major scale the easy way. To separate the notes and play the scale in the regular way is now a simple matter. We have accomplished something. To play scales with many sharps should not necessarily create problems.

This is where we stop: do not attempt to go on yet to the next two scales, F# and C# major; the student will learn to play them at a later date. Only when he is thoroughly at home with B major and can play it without looking at his hands, should he proceed to F# and C# major and learn to play them like any other scales. But, at this early stage, and since the thumb has to find its place always on a different white key, it may cause confusion.

The young student should certainly be taught the correct theoretical development of the scales, the sooner the better, and by all means before we start teaching the flat scales.

A beginner's scale will not sound smooth, and the thumb will need the instructor's special attention. Let four to six weeks go by before introducing the student to his first exercise, the thumb study. Use the first four lines of Exercise No. 1, page 22, anchoring only the second finger and not extending the stretch beyond the interval of a third. This is easy to remember, and the instructor can teach it without having to write it out.

I do not believe in studies or etudes that require more concentration on the notes than on the keys and fingers. A good teacher will find the student's weakness and help him to overcome it; some students' fingers may be weaker than others. Good exercises are recommended in the chapter concerning the accent. As we do not intend to overtax students or let this become drudgery, we may shorten all exercises.

The student should have a rhythmic concept of the exercises and pieces he is playing. Therefore, time should be given to the analysis and clapping of the patterns before performing at the keyboard. A student can never be taught too early to listen to the sounds he is producing, to attentively listen to his own playing.

Sight-reading and duet playing should also be cultivated. For this purpose a certain amount of time should be set aside during the lesson. This should encourage the student to sight-read on his own; many a good sight-reader has developed in this way. It is essential that the instructor supervise the young student's sight-reading for a certain time, or he may easily get into bad habits and become careless.

As soon as the student is advanced enough, he should learn little pieces by Haydn, Mozart, Bach, Schumann, Beethoven, Bartók, Kabalevsky, Bloch and others. This is the time to discuss their different styles. The student should learn that the Romantic period requires different interpretation from the classic or contemporary styles.

Music teachers may be confronted with many situations that demand much good judgment and common sense. There is nothing unusual in students having fingernails bitten to the quick; the instructor must consider this, for in such a case it is painful to depress the key at a certain angle.

The instructor learns to make the right decision if common sense becomes his guide.

There is no end of learning.

Robert Schumann
Rules for Young Musicians

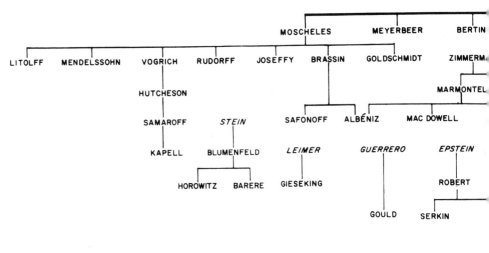

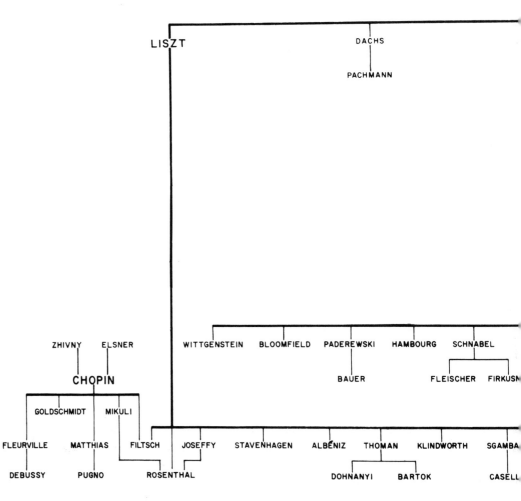

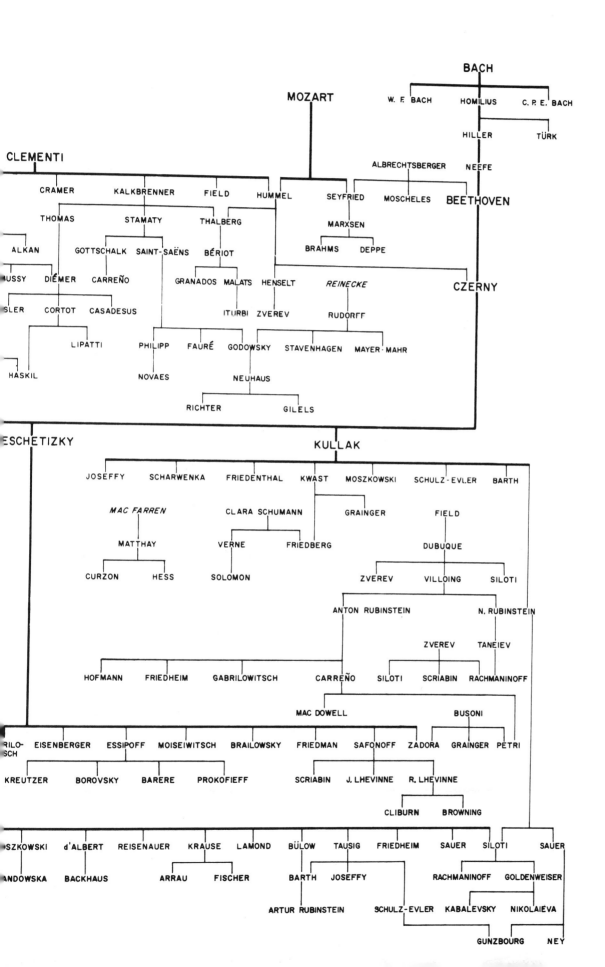

Albéniz, Isaac	1860-1909	Gabrilowitsch, Ossip	1876-1936	Neefe, Christian Gottlob	1748-1798
d'Albert, Eugen	1864-1932	Gieseking, Walter	1895-1956	Neuhaus, Heinrich	1888-1964
Albrechtsberger, Johann	1736-1809	Gilels, Emil	1916	Ney, Elly	1882-1968
Alkan (Morhange), Charles H.V.	1813-1888	Godowsky, Leopold	1870-1938	Nikolaieva, Tatjana	1924
Arrau, Claudio	1904	Goldenweiser, Alexander	1875-1961	Novaes, Guiomar	1895-1979
		Goldschmidt, Otto	1829-1907		
Bach, Carl Philipp Emanuel	1714-1788	Gottschalk, Louis Moreau	1829-1869	Pachmann, Vladimir de	1848-1933
Bach, Johann Sebastian	1685-1750	Gould, Glenn	1932	Paderewski, Ignace Jan	1860-1941
Bach, Wilhelm Friedemann	1710-1784	Grainger, Percy Aldridge	1882-1961	Petri, Egon	1881-1962
Backhaus, Wilhelm	1884-1973	Granados, Enrique	1867-1916	Philipp, Isidor	1863-1958
Barere, Simon	1896-1951	Guerrero, Alberto	1886-1959	Prokofieff, Serge	1891-1953
Barth, Karl Heinrich	1847-1922	Gunzbourg, Mark	1876-1959	Pugno, S. Raoul	1852-1914
Bartók, Béla	1881-1945				
Bauer, Harold	1873-1951	Hambourg, Mark	1879-1960	Rachmaninoff, Sergei	1873-1943
Beethoven, Ludwig van	1770-1827	Haskil, Clara	1895-1960	Reinecke, Carl Heinrich	1824-1910
Bériot, Charles Wilfrid de	1833-1914	Henselt, Adolf von	1814-1889	Reisenauer, Alfred	1863-1907
Bertini, Benoît Auguste	1798-1876	Hess, Dame Myra	1890-1965	Richter, Sviatoslav	1914
Bloomfield-Zeisler, Fanny	1863-1927	Hiller, Johann Adam	1728-1804	Risler, Edouard	1873-1923
Blumenfeld, Felix	1863-1931	Hofmann, Josef	1876-1957	Robert, Richard	1861-1924
Borovsky, Alexander	1889-1968	Homilius, Gottfried August	1714-1785	Rosenthal, Moriz	1862-1946
Brahms, Johannes	1833-1897	Horowitz, Vladimir	1904	Rubinstein, Anton	1829-1894
Brailowsky, Alexander	1896-1976	Hummel, Johann Nepomuk	1778-1837	Rubinstein, Artur	1886
Brassin, Louis	1840-1884	Hutcheson, Ernest	1871-1951	Rubinstein, Nicholas	1835-1881
Browning, John	1933			Rudorff, Ernst	1840-1916
Bülow, Hans von	1830-1894	Iturbi, José	1895-1979		
Busoni, Ferruccio	1866-1924			Safonoff, Vassily	1852-1918
		Joseffy, Rafael	1852-1915	Saint-Saëns, C. Camille	1835-1921
Carreño, Maria Teresa	1853-1917			Samaroff, Olga	1882-1948
Casadesus, Robert Marcel	1899-1972	Kabalevsky, Dmitri	1904	Sauer, Emil von	1862-1942
Casella, Alfredo	1883-1947	Kalkbrenner, Friedrich Wilhelm	1788 1849	Scharwenka, Franz Xaver	1850-1924
Chopin, Frédéric Francois	1810-1849	Kapell, William	1922-1953	Schnabel, Artur	1882-1951
Clementi, Muzio	1752-1832	Krause, Martin	1853-1918	Schulz-Evler, Andrey	1852-1905
Cliburn, Van	1935	Kreutzer, Leonid	1884-1953	Schumann, Clara	1819-1896
Cortot, Alfred	1877-1962	Kullak, Theodor	1818-1882	Scriabin, Alexander	1872-1915
Cramer, Johann Baptist	1771-1858			Serkin, Rudolf	1903
Curzon, Clifford	1907	Kwast, James	1852-1927	Seyfried, Ignaz Xaver von	1776-1841
Cutner, Solomon	1902			Sgambati, Giovanni	1841-1914
Czerny, Carl	1791-1857	Lamond, Frederic	1868-1948	Siloti, Alexander	1863-1945
		Landowska, Wanda	1877-1959	Solomon, *see Cutner*	
Dachs, Joseph	1825-1896	Leimer, Karl	1859-1944	Stamaty, Camille Marie	1811-1870
Debussy, Claude	1862-1918	Leschetizky, Theodor	1830-1915	Stavenhagen, Bernhard	1862-1914
Deppe, Ludwig	1828-1890	Lhévinne, Josef	1874-1944	Stein, Theodor	1819-1893
Diémer, Louis	1843-1919	Lhévinne, Rosina	1880-1976		
Dohnanyi, Ernst von	1877-1960	Lipatti, Dinu	1917-1950	Taneiev, Sergius	1856-1915
Dubuque, Alexander	1812-1898	Liszt, Franz	1811-1886	Tausig, Carl	1841-1871
		Litolff, Henry Charles	1818-1891	Thalberg, Sigismond	1812-1871
Eisenberger, Severin	1879-1945			Thoman, Stefan	1862-1940
Elsner, Joseph Xaver	1769-1854	Mac Dowell, Edward	1861-1908	Thomas, C.L. Ambroise	1811-1896
Epstein, Julius	1832-1918	Mac Farren, Walter	1826-1909	Türk, Daniel Gottlob	1756-1813
Essipoff, Anna	1851-1914	Malats, Joaquim	1872-1912		
		Marmontel, Antoine François	1816-1898	Verne, Mathilde	1865-1936
Fauré, Gabriel Urbain	1845-1924	Marxsen, Eduard	1806-1887	Villoing, Alexander	1804-1878
Field, John	1782-1837	Matthay, Tobias	1858-1945	Vogrich, Max Wilhelm	1852-1916
Filtsch, Károly	1830-1845	Matthias, Georges Amadée St.C.	1826-1910		
Firkusný, Rudolf	1912	Mayer-Mahr, Moritz	1869-1947	Wittgenstein, Paul	1887-1961
Fischer, Edwin	1886-1960	Mendelssohn-Bartholdy, Felix	1809-1847	*(Left hand piano virtuso)*	
Fleischer, Leon	1923	Meyerbeer, Giacomo	1791-1864		
Fleurville, Mme. Mauté de	1823-1883	Mikuli, Karl	1821-1897	Zadora, Michael von	1882-1946
Friedberg, Carl	1872-1955	Moiseiwitsch, Benno	1890-1963	Zhivny (Żywny) Adalbert	1756-1842
Friedenthal, Albert	1862-1921	Moscheles, Ignaz	1794-1870	Zimmerman, Pierre Joseph	1785-1853
Friedheim, Arthur	1869-1932	Moszkowski, Moritz	1854-1925	Zverev, Nikolai	1832-1893
Friedman, Ignaz	1882-1948	Mozart, Wolfgang Amadeus	1756-1791		